AF270559

THE SACRAMENT

A Historical View

LEE H. VAN DAM

THE SACRAMENT – A Historical View

Art by Cary Averett
Book layout by Robyne Gallacher

Published in the United States by
LHVD Books
Cottonwood Heights, Utah
www.lhvdbooks.com

ISBN: 978-0-9903610-5-3

Library of Congress Control Number 2022904236

Also by the author

Cruising – A View Through the Porthole
Golfing – A View Through the Golf Hole
Hong Kong – A View of a Remarkable City

Contents

Preface

For many years, I have been interested in the history of the sacrament in this dispensation. While serving as a young missionary for The Church of Jesus Christ of Latter-day Saints, I remember creating a special folder in which I placed information concerning the sacrament – talks, articles, stories, anecdotes, quotes, and such. Eventually that small folder, which grew thicker and thicker over time, was replaced by a number of larger folders and binders about the sacrament.

This book is my attempt to put in writing some of the things I have learned about the sacrament and its fascinating history. As I do so, I wish to express my appreciation to the many people whose meaningful articles, talks, insights, stories, and comments about the sacrament have influenced the contents of this book.

I hope you enjoy reading it. Writing it has been a marvelous experience for me.

- Lee H. Van Dam

Three Special Sacrament Services

Wouldn't it have been a wonderful privilege to have been in attendance at three of the most significant sacrament services ever held? All sacrament services are special, but in my mind, three of the most meaningful ones in history were the Last Supper, the time that Jesus Christ first administered the sacrament to the Nephites, and the meeting on April 6, 1830 where the Church of Jesus Christ of Latter-day Saints was organized and the sacrament was first administered in this dispensation.

The Last Supper

Although the term Last Supper doesn't appear in the scriptures, many people, Christians and non-Christians alike, know to some extent what is meant by the expression. Through the scriptures, and because of the many talks, books, articles, and lessons on the subject, **we, as members of The Church of Jesus Christ of Latter-day Saints, are privileged to have an especially wonderful understanding of the Last Supper and its significance.** Among the many accounts of this event, I particularly like the way Elder James E. Talmage described the Last Supper in his book *Jesus the Christ*. On pages 596 and 597, he writes:

"While Jesus with the Twelve sat at table, He took a loaf or cake of bread, and having reverently given thanks and by blessing sanctified it, He gave a portion to each of the apostles, saying: 'Take, eat; this is my body.' Then, taking a cup of wine, He gave thanks and blessed it, and gave it unto them with the command: 'Drink ye all of it; for this is my blood of the new testament, which is shed for many for the remission of sins.' In this simple but impressive manner was instituted the ordinance, since known as the Sacrament of the Lord's Supper."

This first-ever sacrament service, held in a plain upper room in Jerusalem, **provided the pattern we follow today in our sacrament services** – a pattern of reverence, sanctity, and thanksgiving as we remember the life and Atonement of Jesus Christ.

Christ's Visit to the Nephites

The introduction to the Book of Mormon says, **"The crowning event recorded in the Book of Mormon is the personal ministry of the Lord Jesus Christ among the Nephites soon after His resurrection."** As recorded in 3 Nephi, one of the most significant things that Jesus did while visiting the multitude in the land Bountiful was to institute the sacrament. In Chapter 18 we read that Jesus commanded his disciples to bring bread and wine to Him. He took the bread and blessed it and gave it to the disciples and the multitude. He then did the same with the wine. He instructed them that they should always observe to do this in remembrance of the body He had shown them and the blood that He had shed for them. **He promised that if they partook of the bread and wine in remembrance of Him, they would always have His Spirit with them.**

A day later, as recorded in Chapter 20, Jesus returned and administered the sacrament a second time. He told the multitude, "He that eateth this bread eateth of my body to his soul; and he that drinketh of this wine drinketh of my blood to his soul; and his soul shall never hunger nor thirst, but shall be filled. Now when the multitude had all eaten and drunk, behold, they were filled with the Spirit; and they did cry out with one voice, and gave glory to Jesus, whom they both saw and heard."

The Organization of the Church

April 6, 1830 was a remarkable day. After nearly 2,000 years, the authorized Church of Jesus Christ was restored to the earth. The meeting to officially organize the Church was held on **Tuesday, April 6, rather than on a Sunday,** in order to honor and commemorate the birth of our Savior Jesus Christ on April 6. The book *Saints, the Standard of Truth* says the following on page 84 about that special day:

"On April 6, 1830, Joseph and Oliver met in the Whitmer home to follow the Lord's commandment and organize His church. To fulfill the requirements of the law, they chose six people to become the first members of the new church. Around forty women and men also crowded into and around the small home to witness the occasion."

After the meeting was opened, Joseph Smith and Oliver Cowdery were sustained by those in attendance, after which Joseph laid his hands on the head of Oliver and ordained him an elder in the church. Then Oliver ordained Joseph. Continuing on page 85 of *Saints*, we read:

"Afterward, they (Joseph and Oliver) administered the bread and wine of the sacrament in remembrance of Christ's Atonement. They then laid hands on those who had been baptized, confirming them members of the church and giving them the gift of the Holy Ghost. The Lord's Spirit was poured out on those in the meeting, and some in the congregation began to prophesy. Others praised the Lord, and all rejoiced together."

Conclusion

I am grateful for these three special occasions when the sacrament was administered – in Jerusalem, in the land Bountiful, and in the Whitmer home. **As I ponder these accounts, I am impressed with the sanctity and deep meaning of the sacrament ordinance.** I am also impressed with its simplicity.

How grateful I am for the restored gospel, for modern-day revelation, and for the precious opportunity we have to partake of the sacrament each Sunday in remembrance of the remarkable Atonement of the Lord Jesus Christ. **I love the Savior and am profoundly grateful for His love for me and for His sacrifice in my behalf.**

Sacrament Term

Cenacle

The Cenacle (pronounced sen′i kəl) is the traditional site in Jerusalem where many Christians believe the upper room is located – the room in which the Last Supper took place and where Christ instituted the sacrament. The word cenacle comes from Latin and means dining room. The Cenacle is located outside the current walls of Jerusalem in an area called Mt. Zion. During Christ's time, this region was part of the city of Jerusalem.

The scriptures make reference in two places **(Mark 14:15-16 and Luke 22:12-13)** to an upper room being the location of the events of the Last Supper. In Mark we read, "And he will shew you a large upper room furnished and prepared: there make ready for us. And the disciples went forth, and came into the city, and found as he had said unto them: and they made ready the passover."

If you have the opportunity of taking a tour of the holy sites while visiting Jerusalem, your guide will probably take you to visit the Cenacle. **It is a large room with ornate Gothic pillars and a high vaulted ceiling.** It is located in the King David's Tomb compound.

There is considerable debate among scholars concerning whether or not this is the actual room where the Last Supper took place.

(Note – Many Christians also claim that the Cenacle is the location where the Holy Spirit descended on the disciples on the day of Pentecost.)

Frequency of the Sacrament Ordinance

I've enjoyed belonging to a Church that, as my father used to say, "has its head on straight." **Our Church knows what it is doing and it knows where it is going.** I appreciate our clear scriptures, our unified leadership, our orderly temples, our correlated teaching system, our well-defined missionary program, our meetings that start and end on time (kind of), and our inspired *General Handbook* that guides so much of what we do.

These well-organized and orderly things that we are accustomed to in today's Church didn't, of course, just blossom into full maturity right from the start. Most of the things that make up the Church as we know it, started out small and grew gradually until they became what we have today. It has been that way with the sacrament as well. **We didn't just organize the Church in 1830 and then immediately begin holding sacrament meetings each Sunday in meetinghouses.**

Let me share with you some of the things I discovered during my research about the frequency of the sacrament and the growth of its use in the Church. (Note – I am indebted to Justin R. Bray who wrote the excellent article, *The Lord's Supper in Early Mormonism*, and William G. Hartley for his scholarly study

8

entitled, *Mormon Sundays*. Their writings provided a great deal of helpful information about the frequency of the sacrament.)

- **Waiting Until the Church was Organized** – Even though the priesthood had been restored nearly a year earlier in 1829, and the exact sacrament prayers had already been given to us as the Book of Moroni was translated (see Moroni 4:3 and 5:2), the Lord waited until the meeting in the Peter Whitmer home on Tuesday, April 6, 1830, before having Joseph Smith introduce the sacrament ordinance to the Saints.

- **The Sacrament on the Sabbath Day** – The next record we have of the sacrament being administered in this dispensation was on Wednesday, June 9, 1830, two months after the Church was organized. The occasion was the first conference of the Church and the location was again in the Whitmer home. It appears that the Church did not institute a formal regular weekly sacrament service on Sundays until sometime after that. **Sunday was not designated in the scriptures as the day to meet and have the sacrament until August 7, 1831 (as recorded in Doctrine and Covenants 59:12), some 16 months after the Church was organized.** At that time, the Church was told: "But remember that on this, the Lord's day, thou shalt offer thine oblations and thy sacraments unto the Most High…"

- **Sporadic Sacrament Services** – Because of the persecution Church leaders and members faced and the frequent uprooting of the Church during its early years, the sacrament took place when occasion permitted, which was somewhat sporadically.

- **Not Always the Primary Focus at First** – Much of the time spent in early worship services focused on preaching the doctrines of the restoration and organizing the infant Church. In many instances during those years, although the sacrament was administered and it was important, it was not always the primary purpose of the meeting and the meeting was not always called a sacrament meeting, as such. In fact, the sacrament was customarily the last part of the meeting. Talks were often given leading up to (and even during) the sacrament ordinance, with the Lord's Supper being the conclusion of the meeting.

- **As Membership Grew** – Church meetings became more formal and organized as the Church grew and the congregations got larger. As this happened, the sacrament was served more regularly and the method of administering it became more consistent from congregation to congregation.

- **In Kirtland** – After the main body of the Church relocated to Kirtland, regular Sunday sacrament services were the norm. They were typically held in homes, one-room schoolhouses, or outdoors when the weather permitted. At the dedication of the Kirtland Temple on Sunday, March 27, 1836, the sacrament was distributed to the congregation. **About that experience, it was recorded that the congregation was thrilled by the sacred ritual.** On April 3, 1836, a week after the Kirtland Temple had been dedicated, the sacrament was again served as part of the Sabbath day meeting held in the temple. After distributing the Lord's Supper, Joseph Smith and Oliver Cowdery received the marvelous vision recorded in Section 110 of the Doctrine and Covenants. Thereafter, it became the practice for the sacrament to be administered to large numbers in the Kirtland Temple on most Sabbath days.

- **Outside of Church Headquarters** – Outside of Church headquarters, the sacrament was less frequent, being provided only when conditions were favorable to do so. Records indicate that some early wards administered the sacrament only once per month. An example of this was in Iowa in the 1840s where a group of Saints decided to only have the sacrament on the second Sunday of each month. This type of independent policy making was not uncommon during the early years of the Church.

- **During the Nauvoo Period** – Sacrament meetings were a normal weekly event during the Nauvoo period, often with

10

meetings being held outdoors (such as in an outdoor grove of trees not far from the temple site). Once construction progressed to allow for meetings to be held in the temple, the sacrament ordinance was often part of those meetings.

- **While Crossing the Plains** – Sacrament meetings were held on Sundays whenever possible as the Saints rested for the day during their treks across the plains. Some pioneer journals indicate that holding two Sabbath-day meetings was the custom – a worship service in the morning and a meeting at which the sacrament was served later in the day.

- **Valley Wide Sacrament Meetings** – Once the Saints were settled in the Salt Lake Valley and had completed the construction of the "old" tabernacle in 1852 (which was replaced in 1867 by the "new" tabernacle we still use today), valley wide sacrament meetings were often held in those buildings on Temple Square on Sundays.
- **In the Sunday Schools** – With the introduction of the sacrament in the Sunday Schools of the Church in 1877, the

sacrament became much more broadly available – twice each Sunday for those members, young and old, who attended both Sunday School and sacrament meeting. This practice of having the sacrament twice each Sunday **continued for 103 years** until the three-hour block of meetings came into being in 1980. Since then, the sacrament has been served just once each Sunday throughout the Church.

- **Dedication of the Salt Lake Temple** – The first dedicatory service of the Salt Lake Temple was on Thursday, April 6, 1893. The sacrament was served in the temple on that occasion – and thereafter as part of many other meetings held in the Salt Lake Temple over the years.

- **Since the Early 1900s** – Since the early 1900s, as Latter-day Saint communities have become more established and stable and as the Church has spread into more nations around the globe, our Sunday worship has become more regular and standardized, with weekly sacrament meetings taking place in all wards and branches. During this period, by way of talks, magazine articles, bulletins, and letters sent to Church leaders, the Church has provided more and more guidelines and instructions pertaining to the holding of sacrament meetings and the proper procedures to follow for the administration of the sacrament in those meetings. Today's *General Handbook* contains a number of pages covering sacrament meetings and the sacrament ordinance. This has led to great consistency throughout the Church. Whether you attend church in Asia, South America, Europe, the Pacific, Africa, or elsewhere, you will find uniform sacrament meetings wherever you go that have similar and consistent ways of administering the sacrament.

In Conclusion

As the Church was organized in April 1830, the Lord said, **"It is expedient that the church meet together often to partake of bread and wine in the remembrance of the Lord Jesus**

(Doctrine and Covenants 20:75).” Although, as members of the Church, we meet frequently for a variety of purposes (after all, we are known as a meeting-going people), **the most important meeting we have is our sacrament meeting where we can reflect on Christ's Atonement and renew our covenants.** What a great blessing that weekly sacrament meeting is in our lives!

(Note – Perhaps some of you will remember, as I do, that years ago brief sacrament meetings were even held in our meetinghouses on Sunday evenings after the conclusion of general conference as well as on Sunday evenings after our quarterly stake conferences.)

Sacrament Term

Eucharist

The term **Eucharist** is the word used in some Christian denominations to denote the sacrament. Members of those churches who partake of the sacramental bread or wafer and the sacramental wine, usually at an altar or communion table, are known as **communicants.** Their participation in this rite is referred to as **"celebrating the Eucharist"** or **"receiving the Eucharist."** The word Eucharist has its origin in the Greek word *eucharistia,* which means thanksgiving.

Today, the Roman Catholic, Eastern Orthodox, Oriental Orthodox, Anglican, and Presbyterian churches are among those who use the word Eucharist, while most Protestant and evangelical denominations rarely use the term. Instead, they refer to it as the Lord's Supper, Breaking Bread, or Holy Communion.

In The Church of Jesus Christ of Latter-day Saints, we call it the sacrament.

10, 9, 8, 7...Sacrament in Space

Astronaut Don Lind partook of the sacrament while traveling 17,500 miles per hour in space; **Corporal Royal Meservy** had the sacrament while being held prisoner in Stalag IX-B in Germany; **Commander Kelly Laing** partook of the sacrament below the surface of the ocean while serving on a nuclear submarine; and **quarterback Steve Young** held sacrament services in his hotel room on Saturday evenings. Let's take a look at the stories behind these four special sacrament experiences.

Astronaut Don Lind

Don Lind partook of the sacrament while traveling in space on the Space Shuttle Challenger. On Sunday, May 5, 1985, Don was aboard the shuttle orbiting the earth at an altitude of approximately 207 miles. At an average speed of 17,500 miles per hour, the space shuttle orbited the earth every 90 minutes. He and the other six members of the astronaut crew saw 16 sunrises and 16 sunsets each day they were in space. They spent a total of 7 days, 8 minutes, and 46 seconds on the Challenger during their journey.

Don had prepared well for his trip into space. Born in Midvale, Utah in 1930, he graduated from Jordan High School in Salt Lake City and earned a Bachelor of Science degree with high honors in Physics in 1953 from the University of Utah. Don then

attended the U.S. Navy Officer Candidate School where he received training as a Naval aviator, and followed that by earning a Ph.D. in Physics at Berkley.

As Brother Lind was selected to be an astronaut and assigned to be part of the Challenger 7 crew, he realized that their mission would cover a full week and that he would be in space on the Sabbath. **Don visited with his bishop and received permission to hold his own sacrament service while on board the shuttle.** This presented him both a special opportunity – and an unusual challenge. Here is Brother Lind's account of the situation as he spoke at the invitation of the First Presidency in the October 1985 priesthood session of general conference:

"An experience that was very close to me was to have the sacrament in orbit. We were in space for a full week, so, of course, we were up there on a Sunday. Our bishop had given me permission to hold my own sacrament service. It was a little unusual. You priests in the audience might consider what it would be like to try to kneel down in weightlessness – you keep drifting off. **For privacy I held my own sacrament service in my sleep station – something like a Pullman berth. I kneeled on what you would think of as the ceiling and braced my shoulders against my sleeping bag so I would not float away. It was a very special experience.** I will remember that sacrament service and the renewing of my baptismal covenants high above the earth all my life. It had some of that special feeling that you usually have only when you go to the temple."

Concerning Don's visit to space in 1985, here are several additional things about it that I find quite interesting:

- The Triple Combination that Don took with him into space **was presented as a gift to the First Presidency** after his return to earth.
- Don's space shuttle crew was made up of seven individuals. One of them was **the first Chinese person to go into space** (Taylor Gun-Jin Wang who was born in Jiangxi, China) and one was **the first Dutch person to travel into space** (Lodewijk van den Berg who was born in Sluiskil, the Netherlands).
- The Space Shuttle Challenger was the shuttle that experienced a tragic explosion eight months later that killed all crew members on board shortly after its launch on **January 28, 1986.**
- Don Lind's mission carried a satellite into space that was made in Utah in a joint project between Weber State University and Utah State University. **It was called NUSAT (Northern Utah Satellite) and its purpose was to help optimize radar antennas for air traffic control installations.**

- Onboard the shuttle was an experiment involving two squirrel monkeys and 24 rats, all housed in special cages. **Concerning this, NASA liked to joke with the crew that they were on an extra-special mission because of the unusually large number of mammals on board – 33 of them, including the seven astronauts.**

Corporal Royal Meservy

Corporal Royal R. Meservy served in the 106th Golden Lion Division during World War II. **He was captured during the Battle of the Bulge on December 19, 1944 and spent the rest of the war in Stalag IX-B, a prisoner of war camp in Germany.** While in the POW camp, the soldiers who were members of the Church obtained permission to hold Sunday services and to have the sacrament. Here is Corporal Meservy's recounting of their special Sunday services:

"I was chosen to be the leader of the group and was given the responsibility to organize sacrament and other meetings. **From our meager bread ration we received the night before, we took turns saving a piece about one-half inch wide and three inches long for sacrament bread. We were starved and so weak and tired, but the spirit was strong.** In those terrible times, I'd lie and talk to God as I would my father. I told Him if He'd help me so that I could stay alive, go home, get married, and raise a family, I'd do whatever He or His servants asked me to do. Heavenly Father kept His part of the bargain, and I'm trying to keep my part." (From *Saints at War* by Robert C. Freeman and Dennis A. Wright, pages 153-154)

Commander Kelly Laing

U.S. Navy Commander Kelly Laing has served on four submarines during his career as a Naval officer. **At the time of this writing, Brother Laing is the commanding officer of the USS**

Maine nuclear submarine. With a home port of Bangor, Washington, the USS Maine is a 560-foot ballistic missile submarine that can travel up to 29 miles per hour and dive to a depth of 800 feet. A returned missionary, Brother Laing told the *Church News* (January 11, 2020) about having the sacrament while underwater out at sea:

> "We had some members of the Church on board and I was given permission to hold Church services. During one deployment in a remote stretch of the North Pacific, we were required to be at periscope depth at the same time as the Church gathering. The conditions were horrible. All of us were kneeling around the table and we had to hold onto the sacrament plate and cup to keep them from falling off. **We were getting tossed from side to side while we were blessing the sacrament, but the Spirit was so strong. The conditions were not ideal, but the Spirit was present. That was what mattered.** After the sacrament, our conversation that day focused on the story of the Master when he calmed the seas."

Quarterback Steve Young

Steve Young, the Hall of Fame NFL quarterback who led the San Francisco 49ers to victory in Super Bowl XXIX, tells about receiving special permission from his bishop to hold private sacrament services in his hotel room on the Saturday evening before away games. He says:

> "My bishop, realizing my situation and knowing that I loved and appreciated the sacrament, gave me authorization to hold a worship service in my hotel room on the night before our away games. Being able to partake of the sacrament and worship Heavenly Father each week was always a special experience for me and several Latter-day Saint teammates who often joined me. As we prepared the sacrament and recited the prayers for the bread and water, **I**

always felt close to the Savior and received a renewed desire each time to live more righteously and to be a proper representative of the Lord." (Steve provided the foregoing information to me by way of email exchanges between the two of us.)

Authorization is Essential

Now, just a few thoughts about the holding of sacrament meetings. **In each of the foregoing stories, note that the holding of the sacrament service had to be specifically authorized in advance.** Although we might be worthy and well-meaning, we are not at liberty to organize our own sacrament service and prepare, bless, and pass the sacrament without approval. This approval must come from one who has the keys to the sacrament ordinance – usually a bishop or a branch president.

The Church's handbook points out that when traveling and away from home, **we should always make a diligent effort to attend our Sunday meetings at a nearby ward or branch** and that sacrament services should not be held as part of family reunions or other outings. **Only in unusual situations – such as those mentioned for Brothers Lind, Meservy, Laing, and Young (and such as COVID) – may bishops give authorization for a sacrament service to be held away from the meetinghouse.**

(Note – In addition to Don Lind's significant sacrament meeting in space, it should be noted that astronauts of other faiths have also had special religious experiences there. For instance, **Edwin "Buzz" Aldrin,** a Presbyterian, **celebrated the first communion in space** just before he and Neil Armstrong touched down on the moon's surface in 1969 and **Sheikh Muszaphar Shukor,** an astronaut from Malaysia, **offered the first Ramadan prayers from orbit** while on the International Space Station in 2007.)

Sacrament Term

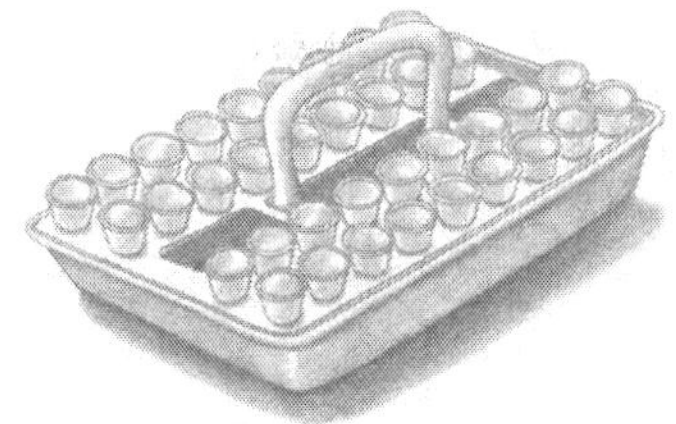

The Lord's Day

As mentioned previously, the scriptures command us to rest from our labors and to worship each week on **"the Lord's day:"**

"But remember that on this, **the Lord's day,** thou shalt offer thine oblations and thy sacraments unto the Most High…" (Doctrine and Covenants 59:12)

We call the **Lord's day,** which we observe once each seven days, **the Sabbath.** The word Sabbath comes from the Hebrew shabbath meaning day of rest. In The Church of Jesus Christ of Latter-day Saints, the day of the week on which most members gather to worship and partake of the sacrament is **Sunday,** the first day of the calendar week. That is our usual Sabbath day.

However, in areas of the world where a country's custom of worship is on a day other than Sunday, the Church authorizes members to meet on that day. Latter-day Saints gather on **Fridays** in most Arab countries such as Jordan, Oman, Morocco, Iraq, Nepal, and Pakistan. Members in Israel hold their weekly sacrament meeting on **Saturday.** In Hong Kong, many members of the Church come from countries such as the Philippines and Indonesia to work as domestic helpers. Because many of their employment contracts do not allow them to have Sunday off as their one day free from work, full Church services are authorized to be held for them **on weekdays.**

No matter which day of the week is involved, we are commanded to observe **the Lord's day** once each seven days in order to rest from our labors, to worship, and to partake of the sacrament.

Do We Trust Them?

Isn't it interesting that we entrust our most sacred ordinance outside of the temple to young men? We give them the tremendous responsibility of blessing, preparing, and passing the sacrament. Adults help train them and provide leadership for them, but we leave the actual hands-on sacrament duties to young people.

Elder Jeffrey R. Holland spoke to this point in 2017 at the National Boy Scout Jamboree held at Summit Bechtel Reserve in West Virginia. **He addressed a group of some 2,100 Latter-day Saint Scouts and leaders in the sacrament meeting that was held there on Sunday, July 23.** Seated in a large outdoor amphitheater, those in attendance had received the sacrament earlier in the meeting **from a group of 180 deacons and 60 priests,** all of whom were Boy Scouts. (That scene brings to mind the special sacrament service in 3 Nephi where Christ provided the sacrament to about 2,500 Nephites.)

In his talk, Elder Holland emphasized the importance of the ordinance by noting **it is repeated in the Church every seven days, to every congregation of any size, and to every man, woman, and child.** He reminded the Scouts and their leaders that the sacrament invokes all other covenants in the Church, including those in the temple.

"And we put it on the backs of teenagers," he said of the Aaronic Priesthood's involvement in the sacrament, asking the youth to consider that "God thinks enough of you to have 12-year-olds pass it, 14-year-olds prepare it, and 16-year-olds bless it."

Having young men involved in the sacrament was not always the case. **In the earlier days of the restored Church, adult men handled most of the sacrament responsibilities.** Occasionally the youth were involved, but their duties at church were typically focused more on the temporal preparation of the building and its surroundings than the sacrament. For instance, in the mid-1870s we find mention in Church records that the responsibilities of deacons included preparing the meetinghouse for worship, ushering, pumping the organ, and hauling fuel. In the 1880s, we find a reference that talks about allowing the deacons to pass the sacrament vessels **"but only if they were sedate, responsible persons."** We also find accounts of adult men administering the sacrament in many wards because people believed that young men could not give proper dignity to the ordinance.

The responsibility for the sacrament gradually began shifting to young men during the latter part of the 1800s. In 1898, Elder Francis M. Lyman of the Quorum of the Twelve Apostles spoke at the Church's first general Sunday School convention. In answer to the question, "Can deacons pass the sacrament?" he answered, **"Certainly, if they are good, steady, worthy deacons they certainly are competent to do it when directed to do so."**

In the early part of the 1900s, in addition to increased sacrament responsibilities, young men were becoming more involved in charitable activities and service work. **In the April 1908 general conference, President Joseph F. Smith requested that the boys of the Lesser Priesthood become more involved in the work.** He said, "Give them something to do that will make them more interested in the work of the Lord, and above all things direct their energies in such a way that they will be helpful to the needy, helpful to the poor, helpful to themselves and to the Church."

A few months later, in June of that year, the General Priesthood Committee of the Church recommended **"that each boy move systematically through Aaronic Priesthood callings."** They suggested fixed age groupings: deacons should be ordained at twelve, teachers at fifteen, priests at eighteen, and elders at twenty-one. Since that time, the Church has established specific ages for ordinations, as shown in the following chart:

Ordination Age Changes

Year	Deacon	Teacher	Priest	Elder
Pre-1908	No set age	No set age	No set age	No set age
1908	12	15	18	21
1925	12	15	17	20
1934	12	15	17	19
1953	12	15	17	20
1954	12	14	16	20
1960	12	14	16	19
1970	12	14	16	18
2019	11+	13+	15+	18

Today, we are blessed to have well-organized Aaronic Priesthood quorums full of young men who are busily engaged in the programs of the Church. **Most of these young men handle the sacrament with dignity and maturity** and are working diligently to prepare themselves to receive the Melchizedek Priesthood and serve missions.

So, to the question, "Do we trust them?" the answer is an emphatic, "Yes, we do!" As Elder Holland concluded his talk to the large congregation of Boy Scouts and leaders at the National Jamboree, he counseled the Scouts to be faithful and to **"step up**

and stiffen your backs" in preparation for the important things that lie ahead for them.

(Note – There are some interesting examples in Church history of very young men being ordained to the Aaronic Priesthood. For instance, in 1849, Apostle Wilford Woodruff was called on a mission which would require him to leave his family for a prolonged time. Before departing, **Elder Woodruff ordained his nine-year-old son,** Wilford, Jr., a priest in the Aaronic Priesthood so that his family would be able to have the sacrament while he was away on his mission.)

(Note – An excellent study of young men and the Aaronic Priesthood is William G. Hartley's, *From Men to Boys: LDS Aaronic Priesthood Offices, 1829-1996*. I recommend it to those who would like a more in-depth look at the subject.)

Sacrament Term

Administer

A little while ago, a discussion was held in our priesthood quorum about the word **administer** as it pertains to the sacrament ordinance. Doctrine and Covenants 20:46 says, "The priest's duty is to preach, teach, expound, exhort, and baptize, **and administer the sacrament.**" A few verses later (verse 58) we read, "But neither teachers nor deacons have authority to baptize, **administer the sacrament,** or lay on hands." We discussed that in these two verses **the word administer refers to breaking the bread and saying the prayers.** (All of this, of course, is always done under the approval of a bishop or branch president).

We also reviewed that, at times, the word **administer** has been used in a broader sense **to apply to the combined sacrament responsibilities of all Aaronic Priesthood holders** (deacons, teachers, and priests) as they provide the sacrament to the congregation, as shown in the following examples:

- The *General Handbook* asks all those who **administer** the sacrament to do so in a dignified manner as they prepare, bless, and pass the sacrament. It also encourages those who **administer** the sacrament to be well groomed and clean. These important guidelines are directed to all Aaronic Priesthood young men, not just priests. (See *General Handbook* Section 18)

- In general conference addresses over the years, general authorities have sometimes used the term **administer** to apply to all members of the Aaronic Priesthood as they fulfill their sacrament responsibilities. For instance, Elder Jay E. Jensen, in the October 2008 **general conference priesthood session** said, "Sabbath after Sabbath, you young priesthood holders **administer** the sacrament to the Saints, who come to sacrament meeting prayerfully, hungering for spiritual healing." (Here, Elder Jensen was directing his remarks to all Aaronic Priesthood holders attending the meeting.)

- When conducting sacrament meeting, a member of the bishopric or branch presidency will often introduce the sacrament ordinance using the word **administer** to mean the entire ordinance, not just what the priests do. He might say, "We will now sing the sacrament hymn, after which the sacrament will be **administered** to the congregation."

And I Love Their Dewy Lips

Selecting the title for this chapter was a bit of a challenge. I wanted a heading that would attract the reader's attention, and felt a catchy phrase from one of the following four sacrament accounts might be good to use. As I read through the stories, I found they contained a number of phrases I quite liked. After evaluating each one, **I picked the dewy lips phrase from the first account.** To me, it was an interesting selection of words that introduced this chapter's subject really well.

Account #1 – And I Love Their Dewy Lips

William A. Hyde, the president of the Pocatello Stake of Zion, wrote the lead article for the May 1911 *Improvement Era.* **It was 13 pages long and the subject was the Lord's Supper.** On the 10th page of his article, he suggested that members of the Church needed to exercise more proper etiquette insofar as drinking from the common sacrament cup was concerned. The entire thirteen-page article is well worth reading, but let me quote just a few sentences from it:

"Another matter, rather more delicate, but which I think ought to be mentioned, concerns the mothers and their babies. I say, bless the babies, for they are the sweetest of all creation, **and I love their dewy lips;** but, you know, all people do not feel that way. An infant does not know how to drink, and until it has learned properly, the (sacrament) cup ought to be withheld from it...The careful mother will see that (the babies) have not been eating cake just before the cup is passed, so that their lips may be free from particles."

Account #2 – The More Fastidious Members Would Twist the Cup

President Spencer W. Kimball turned twelve in 1907, several years before individual sacrament cups were introduced in the Church. In his biography, written by Edward L. and Andrew

E. Kimball, **we read about young Spencer's observations while serving as a deacon:**

> "Because the entire congregation drank from the common goblets, **the more fastidious members would twist the cup** so their lips touched the rim by one of the handles. But this supposedly untouched spot quickly became the most used part of the cup's rim, or so it seemed to the amused deacons."

Account #3 – Still Others Sipped Obediently, Then Wiped Their Lips Vigorously with Handkerchiefs

James L. Jacobs, a member of the Church who lived in Sanpete County, Utah, as a young boy, wrote an essay in the *Saga of the Sanpitch, Volume XV*, pages 8-9, in which he recounted his memories of the sacrament being served **in a quarterly stake conference** held in the early 1900s:

> "There was no problem with the bread. It was prepared on large china plates equipped with high arched handles made of heavy twisted wire and served to the congregation. But the water was another matter. It was served in goblets, which were passed from person to person so each could take a small sip and pass it on to his neighbor and do likewise. Some of the younger ladies did not enjoy drinking from the same container everyone else used. This was especially noticeable when they followed some of the full-bearded old men. Some (of the young ladies) would carefully turn the goblet so they could drink right over the handle. Others placed their hands on each side of the goblet and tipped it up, but did not actually touch their lips to it. **Still others sipped obediently, then wiped their lips vigorously with handkerchiefs** to remove any trace that might have been picked up from previous drinkers."

Account #4 – Abolish This Most Unsanitary Practice

After lab tests found evidence of contagious disease on their ward's sacrament goblets, some members of the Murray 1st Ward, located to the south of Salt Lake City, sent a petition with three pages of signatures to Church headquarters in 1916 that said in part: "We feel that another Sunday should not pass until we can **abolish this most unsanitary practice.**" Interestingly, although many wards in the valley were already using individual cups by then, out in that part of the Salt Lake Valley some were still sharing the goblet. (Note – This petition has been preserved by the Church and is housed in the Church History Department archives.)

A Look Back at the Introduction of Individual Sacrament Cups

With these four short stories helping provide some background, let's look at how individual sacrament cups came to replace the common sacrament goblet in the Church. In the late 1800s and early 1900s, there was growing acceptance among scientists that germs caused disease and that the practice of sharing drinking cups was a health issue. At that time, it was common to find a shared cup or dipper chained to or tied with a strong piece of twine to a drinking fountain in a city square, public park, train car, or even in a school. Bit by bit, at the urging of community officials and health experts, states and municipalities passed laws banning these cups. **But when it came to doing away with the common sacrament cup, our Church's leaders moved slowly – perhaps for two main reasons.** First, Christ and the apostles shared a single cup at the Last Supper and Church leaders were hesitant to deviate from the pattern the Savior had set; and second, many in the Church believed that the blessing pronounced by the priesthood on the water would thwart the transmission of any germs, even if the cup was used by multiple people.

During that period of time, one particular member of the Church stood out in taking a leading role in seeing what could be done about eliminating the common cup and changing to individual sacrament cups. **This was Brother Selden Clawson, an inventor who lived in the Salt Lake 18th Ward.** Noting the growing concern among members of his ward about sharing the common water cup during the sacrament service, Selden brought up the issue in an 18th Ward Sunday School class, and after much discussion on both sides of the subject, a committee was formed to evaluate the idea. The committee studied the issue and felt strongly that individual cups would be an improvement, so they approached their bishop and stake president with their committee's recommendation.

Both the bishop and the stake president agreed with the committee, **but said they did not have the authority to make such a sweeping change to the sacrament ordinance,** so the bishop (Bishop Thomas A. Clawson, who was Selden's half-brother) and Selden were asked by the stake president to visit with general Church leaders about the idea. The two brothers were granted an audience with **President Joseph F. Smith, the president of the Church,** who listened to them and then took the matter to the Council of the Twelve.

On December 15, 1910, the issue was discussed by the leading brethren of the Church **and approval was granted for the 18th Ward to experiment with individual sacrament cups** – but only if the ward paid for the cups themselves.

Based on this approval, Selden Clawson, with the help of several associates, proceeded to make a sacrament set to accommodate individual cups **and on June 18, 1911 in the Salt Lake 18th Ward of the Ensign Stake the first individual sacrament cups were used for the sacrament! The trays were silver and the cups were glass.** The members of Selden's ward loved the results and within the year all wards in the Ensign Stake were using individual cups.

The First Presidency also felt good about the change, and in March 1912 they issued a statement to stake presidents suggesting wards and branches switch to using individual cups. **(Note that the First Presidency only suggested the change, but did not mandate it at this time.)**

Many wards and branches proceeded to make the change to individual cups – **but there was a fair amount of resistance to the idea** – and it took several years for all of the units in the Church to do away with the common sacrament goblet – partially because each local ward was required to raise the money to purchase the new sacrament sets, which were fairly costly.

New Challenges Presented by the Use of Individual Sacrament Cups

As individual cups were authorized and eventually mandated, it was a great blessing to the members of the Church (especially in light of the worldwide Spanish flu epidemic of 1918-1920). But the change didn't come without some new challenges, such as:

- Where can we obtain individual sacrament cups?
- How do we carry the cups to the members of the congregation – i.e., what kind of water trays for individual cups are there and where do we buy them?
- How is the best way to fill the individual cups with water?
- How do we wash and sanitize the cups to make them ready for the next sacrament service?

These challenges, and others, were the genesis for many creative ideas that gave rise to a whole new industry – an industry involved in providing sacrament cups, sacrament trays, water filling devices, and sanitizing systems for the Church to use in its sacrament services. (Please see several other chapters in this book for information about how these challenges were met.)

(Note – For years, a shared drinking cup for all to use was hung on a chain at Salt Lake City's main public water fountain located at the intersection of South Temple and Main Street. Especially on hot summer days, this cup was a much-appreciated courtesy extended to the many residents and visitors who frequented the downtown area, including the Temple Block. **But**

it wasn't until February 1912 that the Utah State Board of Health issued a proclamation banning communal cups in the State of Utah – but, interestingly, the ban exempted cups used in congregations of worship.)

(Note – The beautiful Salt Lake 18th Ward meetinghouse where the first individual cups were used, was built in the 1870s at 107 North A Street in Salt Lake City. In 1973, rather than tearing it down, the entire building was carefully dismantled, moved, and put together again on Salt Lake's Capitol Hill (at 128 East 300 North) across from the Utah State capitol building. This famous old chapel where the first individual sacrament cups were introduced, is now a nonsectarian meeting place used for concerts, weddings, and various other civic functions.)

Sacrament Term

First Communion

First Communion is a tradition observed in some Christian denominations **during which a person receives communion (the sacrament) for the first time.** Practiced by many Catholic and some Protestant churches, First Communion is viewed as an important rite of passage in a person's spiritual life. **It typically takes place between the ages of seven and thirteen.**

First Communion is part of a special mass or church ceremony held in honor of the participants. Those receiving communion for the first time line up and proceed to the front of the church **where a priest or minister administers the sacrament to them individually.** Because of the significance of the occasion and to symbolize purity, girls often wear white dresses and veils and boys wear white suits or jackets. Afterwards, many families host a celebration that includes food, music, photos, and the giving of well wishes and religious-oriented gifts to the young persons.

In The Church of Jesus Christ of Latter-day Saints, we do not observe First Communion. All people, including young children and babies, are welcome to partake of the sacrament for the first time at any age.

White Shirts? Ties?

When participating in the ordinance of the sacrament, what is the proper dress for priesthood holders? **White shirts? Ties? Pants? Shoes?** Let's take a look at this important subject.

Fiji

When my wife and I were vacationing in Fiji, we loved the sacrament meeting we attended one Sunday morning in Suva, the capital city. The meetinghouse, located just a short distance from the temple, was a beautiful building. Its many windows were wide open to let the tropical breezes flow through. The singing by the congregation, all done a cappella, was deep, resonant, and full of spirit! **As we looked around, we noticed that many of the men in attendance, including a number of the deacons, teachers, and priests, were wearing white shirts, ties, – and skirts (called sulus).** A sulu is a traditional Fijian garment, worn by both men and women, that is wrapped around the hips and legs and fastened by tying at the waist.

And then we noticed something that both surprised and impressed us. **One of the deacons who was wearing a white shirt, tie, and sulu, removed his sandals during the sacrament hymn and approached the sacrament table in bare feet at the conclusion of the song.** After the sacrament prayer, he and the other young priesthood holders proceeded to distribute the sacrament to the congregation in a very dignified manner.

After the sacrament meeting, I approached the young man and was able to talk to him and his father. I commented on how reverent the service was and asked the young man, whose name was John, about his taking off his sandals. Speaking for his son because his son didn't speak English, the father simply said, **"John loves the sacrament and wanted to honor the Savior by removing his shoes."**

The Philippines

When we were traveling in the Philippines one time, we attended a wonderful temple session in the Cebu Temple. When I rented temple clothing, they forgot to give me a tie to wear, so I went back and asked for one. The kind lady explained that in the Philippines, **men wore a barong in the temple and that no tie was needed.** A barong, worn by Philippino men on formal occasions, is a beautiful long-sleeved shirt with intricate embroidery on the front that is worn untucked. **Even in the temple, no tie was worn with it.** (Note – Although ties are not required in the temple, priesthood holders in the Philippines do typically wear white shirts and ties when participating in the sacrament.)

Hong Kong

In Hong Kong in the late 1960s, many members of the Church were very poor and had few clothes. As we came to the end of our missions, it was the practice among many of us who were departing for home, **to leave a few of our white shirts and ties behind with the branch president in our last area.** He would then give them to any Aaronic Priesthood boys (or adult men) in the branch who were too poor to have a white shirt and a tie to wear as they participated in the sacrament.

Vietnam

In my files I have a story told by a soldier who fought as an infantryman in the jungles of Vietnam. He tells about how much he loved the sacrament and how he wished he could have observed it in the normal manner each week. But he was the only Latter-day Saint in his unit, didn't have a white shirt and tie, and even if he had had a white shirt, wearing anything white in the jungle would have been very dangerous. **So, he did the best he could under the circumstances.** If he had the opportunity on the Sabbath day, he would quietly kneel **in his khakis**, place the sacrament emblems in his mess kit and canteen cup, and bless and partake of the sacrament.

What is Proper?

What is the proper dress for those who are involved in the sacrament ordinance? **Are white shirts required? Ties? Pants? Shoes?** Let's look at the Church's policies and guidelines over the years concerning this subject.

Members of the Church have always been encouraged to make attendance at church meetings an important event and to wear their best **go-to-meeting clothes** as they worship. For the first century of the Church, the clothing emphasis was concerned mostly with **cleanliness and neatness.** This began to change somewhat in the 1930s, as illustrated by an article in the May 1931 *Improvement Era* that was directed to priesthood holders involved in the sacrament ordinance. (Note – In 1931, the Church had approximately 675,000 members in 21 nations. The large majority of the membership was in the United States.)

On page 417 of the magazine, in a section devoted to priesthood quorum matters, **the leaders of the Granite Stake in Salt Lake City** provided suggestions to the rest of the Church concerning the administration of the sacrament. One of their nine suggestions pertained to the dress worn by Aaronic Priesthood boys:

Suggestion #8 – **"It is suggested that boys participating wear black bow ties and white or light shirts and that they do not wear coats**…This suggestion is optional, but we are very much in favor of it and urge that you try it out. Where it has been used, it is very effective."

Notice that this is **the leadership of a stake,** not the general authorities, who are suggesting the dress code. At this period of time, the Church's *General Handbook* was relatively brief and still being developed. **The general leaders of the Church had not yet included in it a dress code for those participating in the**

sacrament ordinance, so Church units were free to develop their own. Two years later, the April 1933 *Improvement Era* carried a photograph of 16 Aaronic Priesthood young men from the Highland Park Ward of the Granite Stake lined up at the sacrament table. They all were wearing white shirts. They all were wearing black bow ties. They all were wearing dark pants. And they were arranged according to height.

As the Church expanded, a need was seen to provide Church-wide guidelines for the important sacrament ordinance, **so the 1940 Church handbook provided some instructions.** It mentioned that formalism in Church worship should be avoided. **It said that although white shirts and dark ties for the young men are proper, it should not be a requirement that each boy be alike in dress and appearance.** It went on further to indicate that the young men should not be required to assume a particular posture or that they should engage in identical actions while passing the sacrament. It specifically mentioned that carrying the left hand behind the back or walking in a stiff manner was unnecessary. **It cautioned against any actions that could be seen as tending towards a military-type look and procedure.** (Note – In 1940, the Church had grown to about 860,000 members in 24 countries.)

As time went by, additional guidelines for the sacrament ordinance were developed by general Church leadership with the expectation that wards and branches would follow the guidelines **so that the administration of the sacrament would be more uniform throughout the Church.** A significant address on this topic was given by President David O. McKay in the October 1956 priesthood session of general conference. (Note – There were approximately 1.3 million members in 40 nations at the time of his talk. The Church was rapidly becoming a more worldwide Church.) In a portion of his talk, he said the following:

> "I am not going to say much about the dress. We are not a people who look to formality, certainly we do not believe in phylacteries, in uniforms, on sacred occasions, but I do think that the Lord will be pleased with a bishopric if they

will instruct the young men who are invited to administer the sacrament to dress properly. **He will not be displeased if they come with a white shirt instead of a colored one, and we are not so poor that we cannot afford clean, white shirts for the boys who administer the sacrament.** If they do not have them, at least they will come with clean hands, and especially with a pure heart.

I have seen deacons not all dressed alike, but they have a special tie or a special shirt as evidence that those young men have been instructed that **'you have a special calling this morning. Come in your best.'** And when they are all in white, I think it contributes to the sacredness of it."

Today's Church

In the past several decades, many additional statements and guidelines have been given concerning the topic of proper dress for those involved in the sacrament. Let's review two particularly pertinent messages on the subject, one by Elder Jeffrey R. Holland and one by President Dallin H. Oaks, and then let's look at what today's *General Handbook* says.

Elder Jeffrey R. Holland, October 1995

"In that sacred setting (of a sacrament meeting) we ask you young men of the Aaronic Priesthood to prepare and bless and pass these emblems of the Savior's sacrifice worthily and reverently. What a stunning privilege and sacred trust given at such a remarkably young age!...**May I suggest that wherever possible a white shirt be worn by the deacons, teachers, and priests who handle the sacrament.** For sacred ordinances in the Church we often use ceremonial clothing, and a white shirt could be seen as a gentle reminder of the white clothing you wore in the baptismal font and an anticipation of the white shirt you will soon wear into the temple and onto your missions.

That simple suggestion is not intended to be pharisaic or formalistic. We do not want deacons or priests in uniforms or unduly concerned about anything but the purity of their lives. **But how our young people dress can teach a holy principle to us all, and it certainly can convey sanctity."**

Elder Dallin H. Oaks, October 1998

"I will not suggest detailed rules, since the circumstances in various wards and branches in our worldwide Church are so different that a specific rule that seems required in one setting may be inappropriate in another. Rather, I will suggest a principle based on the doctrines.

The principle I suggest to govern those officiating in the sacrament – whether preparing, administering, or passing – is that they should not do anything that would distract any member from his or her worship and renewal of covenants. This principle of non-distraction suggests some common principles.

Deacons, teachers, and priests should always be clean in appearance and reverent in the manner in which they perform their solemn and sacred responsibilities…**All who officiate in the sacrament – in preparing, administering, or passing – should be well groomed and modestly dressed, with nothing about their personal appearance that calls special attention to themselves.** In appearance as well as actions, they should avoid distracting anyone present from full attention to the worship and covenant making that is the purpose of this sacred ordinance."

The *General Handbook*

Today's *General Handbook* contains several pages of guidelines covering the proper administration of the sacrament. It stresses that the young men of the Aaronic Priesthood are representing the Lord. The handbook encourages the bishopric to teach the deacons, teachers, and priests to ponder the Savior's Atonement as they carry out their sacrament responsibilities. **It mentions that they should be well groomed and clean and that they should not wear clothing or jewelry that might detract members in any way.** It says that if the bishop needs to counsel a priesthood holder about these matters, he should do so with love and take into account the person's maturity in the Church. It also says that the passing of the sacrament should be natural and not be overly formal.

Summary

In summary, as with most guidelines and policies in the Church, the ones for the sacrament have evolved over the years and have been adjusted to a growing Church which now embraces a global membership in excess of 16 million people spread across more than 160 nations and territories. These members speak scores of different languages, have many diverse customs, cover a wide economic range, have varying degrees of maturity in the Church – and have different dress modes. **So, today's guidelines from our general leaders take those things into account. They encourage white shirts and ties and teach that they are recommended and always proper – but they do not mandate them.**

(Note – I like how one ward I heard of approached this subject. With the guidance of the bishopric, all of the members of the Aaronic Priesthood came to an agreement that their standard of dress for the sacrament would be white shirts and ties **and that they would help each other dress accordingly.** In order to achieve this, the members of the deacons quorum presidency were assigned to do two things – (1) place a few spare ties in the bishop's office for emergencies, and (2) after first checking with the parents, give a white shirt and tie as a present from the quorum to any young man coming into the Aaronic Priesthood who didn't already have these items.

Sacrament Term

Sacramental Wafer

The type of bread used in Christian sacrament services can vary from religion to religion. Many use regular bread (either leavened or unleavened) while others use special thin unleavened wafers called sacramental wafers.

In some religions, the officiating priest will bless and then eat a portion of a large, round sacramental wafer called a host. (Host is a word derived from Latin meaning sacrificial victim.) This large wafer, perhaps as big as six inches in diameter, is made from pure wheat flour and water. The symbol of a cross is often embossed on it. Smaller versions of the host are offered to those from the congregation who may also wish to partake. These smaller sacramental wafers measure about an inch in diameter and usually have a cross stamped on them as well.

Sacramental wafers used in religious services come from a variety of sources ranging from regular bakeries **to specialized producers who make the wafers according to strict religious specifications.** For instance, some churches specify that only water that has been purified be used, others that no additives be included, and still others require that all those involved in making and baking the sacramental wafers be Christian believers in good standing in the church. Some churches even have the dough blessed or have holy water sprinkled on it before it is baked.

The Church of Jesus Christ of Latter-day Saints does not use sacramental wafers and does not specify the type of bread to be used for sacrament purposes.

Clearly, Accurately, and With Dignity

The instructions to those who say the sacrament prayers are that the prayers should be said **clearly, accurately, and with dignity.** In our own ward, that has been the case in nearly every instance I can think of, and I am proud of our Aaronic Priesthood priests (and Melchizedek Priesthood brethren who assist from time to time) for doing such a fine job with the prayers. **Their careful attention to the prayers adds greatly to the sacrament experience.**

When we review the history of the Church as it pertains to the sacrament, we notice that there has been some uncertainty and inconsistency with a few of the details regarding the sacrament prayers. Let's look at several of the questions and issues that have come up over time so as to help us better understand this important part of our sacrament worship.

Are We to Use the Prayers Found in the Scriptures?

Yes. The sacrament prayers for the bread and water were revealed by the Lord and are found in two places in our scriptures – in Moroni 4:3 (bread) and 5:2 (water) and Doctrine and Covenants 20:77 (bread) and 20:79 (water). The Lord has asked that the prayers be said word for word each time the sacrament is blessed. **You will note that one word in the prayer for the bread is different from what is written in Moroni and what is in the Doctrine and Covenants.** The Book of Mormon version uses the word *hath* near the end of the prayer, while the Doctrine and Covenants version uses the word *has*. The sacrament cards provided by the Church for use at today's sacrament tables use the Doctrine and Covenants wording and have the word *has* on them, so this is generally the version used in our meetings.

Because we have been commanded to "meet together often to partake of bread and wine in the remembrance of the Lord Jesus" (Doctrine and Covenants 20:75), **the sacrament prayers are, no doubt, the most repeated verses of scripture we have in our Church.** They are among the few set prayers we use.

Have We Always Used the Prayers Found in the Scriptures?

No, not always. Even though the sacrament prayers are in the scriptures, there is evidence that those prayers were not always used in the early days of the Church. Many converts to the Church came from other religious backgrounds where set sacrament prayers were not used. **It was not uncommon for wording from their previous faiths to creep in as they blessed the sacrament emblems.** This was especially the case in the mission field and in congregations located away from the center of the Church.

In 1873, Brigham Young reprimanded the Saints for not always using the prayers contained in the scriptures. On Sunday, August 31, 1873, he was delivering a discourse in the Bowery in Paris, Idaho. It was a lengthy sermon with the sacrament being passed to the large congregation while the Prophet was speaking. As this was going on, he said:

> "I will give you a word of counsel here with regard to consecrating the bread and the water, which I want the Saints to remember. When you (addressing the bishops and elders) administer the sacrament, **take this book (the book of Doctrine and Covenants) and read this prayer.** Take

the opportunity to read this prayer until you can remember it. You cannot get up anything that is better, and not even equal to it; and when you read it, read it so that the people can hear you…The people have various ideas with regard to this prayer. **They sometimes cannot hear six feet from the one who is praying, and in whose prayer, perhaps, there are not three words of the prayer that is in the book, that the Lord tells us that we should use.**" (*Journal of Discourses*, Vol 16, page 161)

Over time, memorizing the prayers or reading them word for word from the scriptures, became expected of those administering the sacrament. Especially by the start of the 20th century when more and more young men officiated in the ordinance, it became standard procedure for the prayers to be given just as the Lord had revealed them.

If Errors are Made

All who say the sacrament prayers are striving to say them exactly right. **But what happens if errors are made?** The instructions in the handbook specifically give bishops the responsibility for ensuring the correctness of the prayers. If the one giving the prayer makes a mistake in the wording and corrects it himself, no further correction is needed. If no correction is made, the bishop is to kindly ask him to repeat the prayer. **The bishop is cautioned to use discretion to ensure that doing so does not detract from the ordinance or cause undue embarrassment to the priesthood holder.** If needed, another person at the sacrament table can assist.

It is an important principle for the congregation to remember that once the bishop approves the prayer, regardless of it being worded perfectly, the prayer has been approved by the one holding the keys to the ordinance **and the sacrament is considered to have been blessed.** (This same principle applies to other ordinances, such as baptism. If a baptism prayer is not said correctly or if the baptismal candidate was not actually completely

50

immersed, if the presiding priesthood holder at the service allows the baptism to continue without corrections being made, the baptism is valid.)

My friend Randy's grandson, whose name is Jacob, is a special needs priesthood holder. Jacob was born with a neuromuscular disorder that affects virtually every muscle in his body. The disorder is progressive in nature, causing Jacob increasing difficulty in mobility and speech as he ages. By the time he received the Aaronic Priesthood, Jacob was wheelchair-bound. Despite this, while Jacob was in his Aaronic Priesthood years, he was able to help his quorums with their sacrament responsibilities. **When he was a priest, Jacob's special assignment was to bless the water on Fast Sunday. (He was assigned the prayer on the water because it was the shorter of the two.)**

Although any kind of speaking was a struggle for Jacob and saying the words in the sacrament prayers was specially challenging, he would humbly take his turn to say the prayer on the water. **With his father whispering a few words at a time in his ear, Jacob did his best to repeat them.** His sacrament prayers were very touching, with all in the congregation listening intently to every word. **After the prayer was finished, the bishop would nod his approval and the water would then be passed. Many in the ward often commented that they enjoyed an enhanced spiritual experience whenever Jacob blessed the sacrament.**

Kneeling and Raising Hands

Doctrine and Covenants 20:76 says that an elder or priest is to administer the sacrament "and after this manner shall he administer it – **he shall kneel with the church** and call upon the Father in solemn prayer." When congregations were small, the entire congregation, including all who officiated at the sacrament table, usually knelt together as the sacrament prayers were said. **As congregations grew, the leaders of the Church instituted a policy that only the one offering the prayer is to kneel.** Also, in some congregations in the early years of the Church, it was the practice for the one saying the prayer at the sacrament table to raise one hand to the square or raise both hands during the prayer, as shown in the following grainy late-19th century photo of a meeting in Southern Utah. **The raising of the hand or hands was never a Church-wide practice and has been discontinued.**

The Word "Water" or the Word "Wine?"

As it became increasingly common for water to be used instead of wine at the sacrament table, the word "water," rather than the word "wine," was used in the sacrament prayer. Today's sacrament guidelines specifically instruct the one saying the prayer on the water to use the wording in Doctrine and Covenants 20:79 **and to substitute the word "water" for the word "wine."**

How Many at the Table?

During the early period of the Church, questions would sometimes arise concerning how many should be seated at the sacrament table and if one of them was to be assigned to preside at the table. For many wards, **it was a common practice for three to be at the table with the one in the middle presiding.** As the one presiding, he would stand first and give nods and instructions for the others to stand and proceed with preparing and passing the emblems.

In my ward growing up, we had quite a long sacrament table and a large ward, and we typically used four priests at the table. In branches on my mission, we typically had two at the sacrament table. And during COVID-19, I was alone as I administered the sacrament to my wife in our home. Although there is no specific guideline concerning how many should be at the sacrament table, **the number of priests at the table is usually related to the size of the congregation** so that there will be a sufficient number to administer the sacrament in a timely and efficient manner.

What if a Person Doesn't Hold the Proper Priesthood Office?

While my father was serving as mission president in the Netherlands in the early 1950s, he visited a small branch where there was only one priesthood holder seated at the sacrament table as the meeting was to begin. The newly called branch president quietly walked to a brother seated in the small congregation and asked him to sit at the sacrament table to help bless the sacrament. The good brother left his seat and sat in the vacant chair behind the sacrament table.

Dad realized this man was a deacon, not a priest, so my father, as unobtrusively as possible, approached the man and asked the good brother to return to his seat, which he did. My father then took the brother's place behind the sacrament table.

After the meeting, my father asked the man what his priesthood was. He indicated he was a deacon, **but that he had been taught to be obedient to his leaders in the Church,** and so when the branch president asked him to help at the sacrament table, he knew he should do so.

I wonder how often in the Church this type of mistake has been made without it being noticed and corrected?

Which Prayer is Said First?

We know it is the proper procedure to bless the bread first and then the water, as indicated in the scriptures, but there have been occasions in the history of the Church when the blessing of the water followed directly after the blessing of the bread, **with both emblems then being passed simultaneously to the congregation** – apparently for reasons of efficiency.

In Conclusion

As we finish this chapter on sacrament prayers, let's look at two interesting thoughts about the prayers. One comes from Gary Poll who served for 36 years in the Church Education System teaching seminary and institute. In 1997, in one of his lessons about the sacrament, Brother Poll said that he sometimes wondered if Heavenly Father might have a favorite scripture. He said:

> **"I wonder if Heavenly Father might have a favorite scripture.** If so, it might be the sacrament prayers. He might arrange it so that His people would **hear the scripture often.** He might also have it so that the person uttering the scripture **might be kneeling** as he does so. And he would additionally arrange it so that all who are listening to the scripture would do so **with their eyes reverently closed."**

The second interesting idea about the sacrament prayers was expressed by John S. Tanner in the *Encyclopedia of Mormonism* as he wrote about the sacrament experience being both personal and communal:

> "The sacrament prayers invite **personal** introspection, repentance, and rededication, yet they also are **communal,** binding individuals into congregations who jointly and publicly attest to their willingness to remember Christ. **This shared commitment to become like Christ,**

repeated weekly, defines the supreme aspiration of Latter-day Saint life."

The sacrament prayers are special, holding a central position in our worship. Each time we hear them, they give us a great deal to think about. What a wonderful blessing it is each week to have a sacred time available to us during which we can re-evaluate our lives and recommit ourselves to the Savior and His Atonement.

(Note – Soon after a mission was established in Hong Kong in 1955, a number of important and essential Church words, terms, phrases, prayers, and scriptures were translated into Chinese – such as the name of the Church, the name of the Book of Mormon, the sacrament prayers, the baptismal prayer, and Joseph Smith's account of the First Vision. This allowed for church services and missionary efforts to take place as quickly and effectively as possible while more extensive translating was being done. Years later, some of these early things were retranslated to more correctly conform to the original English version. **In the case of the Chinese sacrament prayers, both were retranslated with each prayer receiving a number of changes (eight for the bread and seven for the water).** I had memorized the prayers in 1966 as a young missionary, but when I returned to Hong Kong in 2006 to serve again, I had to relearn the sacrament prayers – as well as many other things. A similar retranslation of sacrament prayers and Church terms, has, no doubt, happened in other foreign languages as well.)

Sacrament Term

Sacramental Wine

It is the practice of many Christian churches to use wine in their worship services. The wine used by them is typically referred to as **sacramental wine, altar wine, or communion wine.** Produced by the individual churches themselves or by certain wineries, the wine is normally **a pure grape wine** specially made for the sacrament. Most sacramental wines are red to symbolize the blood of Christ. In some churches, only the clergy partake of the wine, while in others the sacramental wine is offered to all who wish to participate.

The Church of Jesus Christ of Latter-day Saints uses water for the sacrament. It has been well over a hundred years since wine has been used.

Sacrament Music

In the summer of 1967, I was transferred to a little fishing village on the back side of Hong Kong Island. I had been a missionary in Hong Kong, which at that time was part of the Southern Far East Mission, for 13 months and was excited for this new assignment. After lugging our belongings up ten flights of stairs to our little top-floor apartment, the first thing my companion and I did was to arrange to meet with the branch president to see what we could do to help the branch. As we visited with him, he explained to us that the branch had many needs, but that the most urgent one was for a pianist. **He said that the quality of the music in the branch meetings was not very good, and he felt that a piano player would be a great benefit to the branch.**

My companion and I made the finding of a piano player our top priority and were soon blessed to find a young man who was not only interested in joining the Church, but who could play the piano as well. Even before his baptism, he began playing in branch meetings, **and overnight the spirit of the branch improved dramatically.**

Concerning the impact that music has in our meetings, the First Presidency's preface to our present hymn book says:

"Inspirational music is an essential part of our church meetings. The hymns invite the Spirit of the Lord,

create a feeling of reverence, unify us as members, and provide a way for us to offer praises to the Lord. Some of the greatest sermons are preached by the singing of hymns."

This is particularly true of our sacrament hymns in sacrament meeting. At the present time in the Church, the directive is that **the sacrament hymn is always to be sung by the congregation and that the hymn that is chosen for the sacrament should refer to the sacrament itself or to the sacrifice of the Savior Jesus Christ.** The *General Handbook* specifies that instrumental music or vocal solos should not replace the hymn and that no music should be played during the sacrament prayer, while the sacrament is being passed, or as a postlude when the sacrament has been completed.

Beginning with the first one in 1835, hymnbooks have been published by the Church which contain authorized and appropriate music for our Church meetings. These hymnbooks have always contained a number of hymns especially appropriate for the sacrament. At first, the hymnbooks didn't have a topical index, but for many years now our books have included an index in the back of the book that indicates which hymns are best suited for various occasions – such as for the sacrament, for a baptism, for Christmas, for funerals, etc. **Today's hymnbook lists 28 hymns that are particularly appropriate for the sacrament.**

Let's take a look at our Church hymnbooks over the years to see what we can learn about the history and background of our sacrament hymns.

- **1835 Collection of Hymns** – In 1830, Emma Smith, the wife of the Prophet, was instructed in Doctrine and Covenants Section 25 to make a selection of sacred hymns for the newly restored Church. That book, called *A Collection of Sacred Hymns, for the Church of the Latter Day Saints,* was printed in Kirtland, Ohio in 1835. The book measured three inches by four and one-half inches and fit in a vest pocket. This hymnal contained the texts for 90 hymns, but no music was included. Thirty-nine of the texts were written by Latter-day Saints. **Three sacrament hymns we use today were in that first hymn book:** (1) *Gently Raise the Sacred Strain*; (2) *He Died! The Great Redeemer Died*; and (3) *O God, the Eternal Father*.

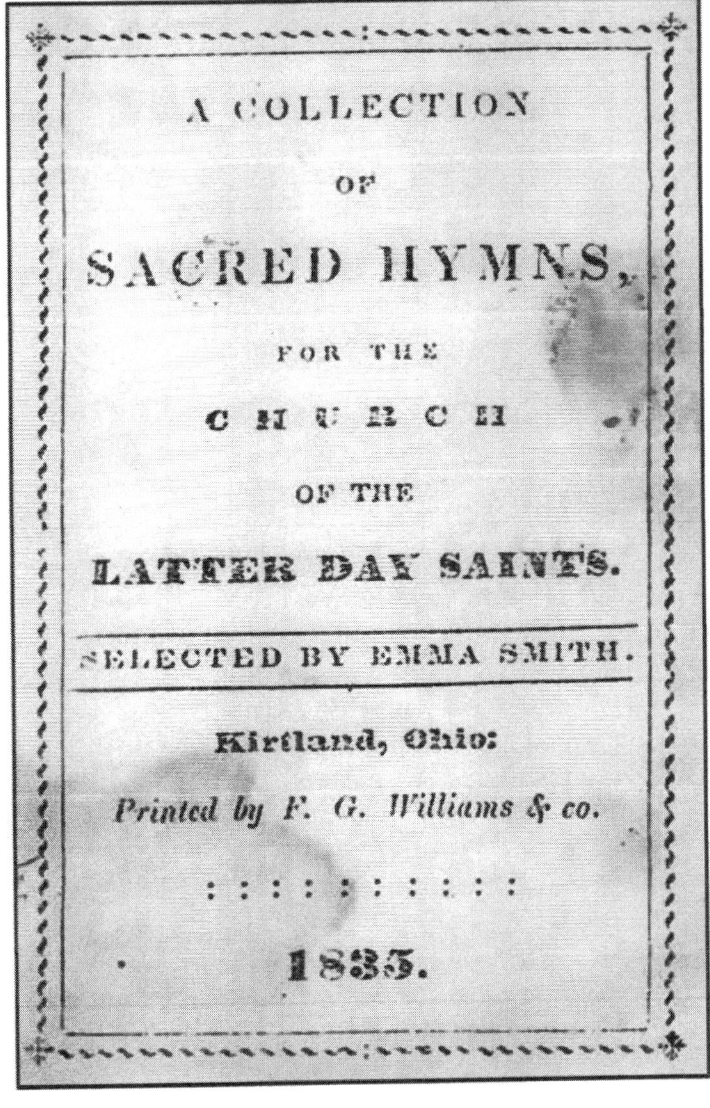

- **Hymn Book Revisions – Every 30 or 40 years, the Church has revised the hymnbook.** As a young boy, the one I grew up with in the Stratford Ward was a blue hymnbook published in 1950. I still remember a little bit of the numbering in that book. Perhaps you remember it as well. *Come, Come, Ye Saints* was hymn #13; *We Thank Thee, O God, for A Prophet* was #196; and *The Spirit of God* was #213.

- **The 1985 Book** – In 1985, the hymnbook we are now using in the Church came out. It is often referred to as the green hymnbook and contains 341 hymns. *Come, Come, Ye Saints* is now hymn #30; *We Thank Thee, O God, for A Prophet* is #19; and *The Spirit of God* is #2. **As mentioned, 28 sacrament hymns are included.** (Note – The chairman of the committee for the 1985 book, Michael Moody, is a friend of ours. For an interesting account of Latter-day Saint hymnbooks over the years, please see his article on the Church website entitled *Latter-day Saint Hymnbooks, Then and Now.*)

- **Hymns Not Retained** – A number of the hymns I remember singing in my youth were not retained in the 1985 book, such as: *Each Cooing Dove; Land of the Mountains High; Shall We Meet Beyond the River;* and *M.I.A., We Hail Thee.* Four sacrament hymns from the previous hymnal were not retained.

- **Most Widely Recognized Hymn** – Perhaps the Church's most widely recognized hymn is because of the Tabernacle Choir at Temple Square. For many years, the choir's introductory hymn, **Gently Raise the Sacred Strain**, which is classified in our hymnbook as a sacrament song, has been heard each week by millions of members and nonmembers throughout the world.

- *I Stand All Amazed* – One of our most beloved sacrament hymns, *I Stand All Amazed*, surprisingly was not written by a member of the Church. Both the music and the text were written by Charles H. Gabriel **who is reputed to have written some 7,000 to 8,000 songs** in his life, most of them religious in nature. Many of his songs appear in church hymnals throughout the Christian world, but of all his thousands of songs, only *I Stand All Amazed* appears in ours.

- **Two Well-known Composers** – Felix Mendelssohn and Johann Sebastian Bach wrote the tunes for two of our sacrament hymns. Mendelssohn wrote the music for *O God, the Eternal Father* and Bach adapted the tune we use for *O Savior, Thou Who Wearest a Crown.*

- **A Very Protestant Hymn** – The music for one of our sacrament hymns, *In Humility, Our Savior*, is used in nearly every Protestant hymnal there is. The hymn tune was written by Rowland Hugh Prichard, a Welsh musician. The words we use with this tune, however, are very Latter-day Saint. Mabel Jones Gabbott, a member of the church, wrote the text.

- **An Opera Song** – Have you ever heard of the opera *The Crusader in Egypt* by Meyerbeer? Neither had I until I discovered that the tune for ***Jesus, Once of Humble Birth*** was adapted from a song from that opera. Giacomo Meyerbeer, a German composer, wrote the little-known opera *Il Crociato in Egitto* (*The Crusader in Egypt*) which was first performed in Venice in 1824.

- **Hymnbook Translations** – Many foreign language translations of the 1985 hymnbook have been made for use around the world. The Church has specific guidelines concerning hymnbook translations. **Typically, each hymnbook in a foreign language will contain approximately 200 hymns.** About one hundred of those are hymns that are required to be in each hymnbook. The remaining hymns are selected by taking into account such things as which hymns have proven to be the most popular in that language, any Christmas hymns that may be different from those used in the English hymnbook, and the national anthems of the countries that speak the translation language.

62

I am grateful for the hymns of the Church and for the young convert in Hong Kong who was able to serve his little branch so well by playing the piano. His talents helped create a more spiritual and reverent atmosphere in the meetings, especially for the sacrament, and were a blessing to all who attended.

As I conclude this chapter, I would like to list **five of my favorite lines** from our sacrament hymns. **Each one carries a powerful message that I personally find very meaningful.** They are:

- "God loved us, so he sent his son." (#187)
- "I stand all amazed at the love Jesus offers me." (#193)
- "His precious blood he freely spilt; His life he freely gave." (#195)
- "Let us remember and be sure, Our hearts and hands are clean and pure." (#173)
- "Grant us, Father, grace divine; May thy smile upon us shine." (#170)

(Note – The Church made an announcement in June 2018 that it was planning to publish a new hymnbook and a new children's songbook that would better suit a worldwide church. Members were invited to submit original sacred music for consideration. Since then, periodic news updates from the Church indicate that thousands of submissions have been received and that the committee hopes to have the new books ready to publish several years from now.)

Sacrament Term

Mood Marking

Each of our Latter-day Saint hymns has a mood marking. In the hymn book or on an electronic device, the mood marking appears on the left side below the hymn number and just above the start of the music. **Mood markings suggest the general feeling or spirit of the hymn.** For instance, the mood markings suggest that *There Is Sunshine in My Soul Today* be sung "joyfully," that *Count Your Blessings* be sung "brightly," and that *Called to Serve* be sung "with conviction."

One of my favorite mood markings for a Church song is in the Children's Songbook. For the wonderful song *Follow the Prophet*, the mood marking is **"with energy."** I'm sure that President Russell M. Nelson concurs with that mood marking.

All of the mood markings for our 28 sacrament hymns suggest they be sung with great reverence, spirituality, and solemnity. **Some of the specific mood markings for our sacrament hymns are "thoughtfully," "prayerfully," "fervently," "with dignity," "worshipfully," and "meekly."**

Other Than Bread and Water

George Q. Cannon served a mission in Hawaii in the early 1850s. He treasured those years as a missionary and loved to tell stories about the wonderful Hawaiian Saints and the experiences he had while laboring among them. Years later, while serving as the first counselor in the First Presidency, President Cannon gave the following thoughts concerning the sacrament emblems:

"There are times and places where the Lord permits, on account of the condition and surroundings of His people, a slight deviation from established customs. For instance, on some of the small islands of the South Pacific Ocean there is no bread, and all the water is salt, and the fruit of the coconut tree is the chief food of man. If the members of the Church waited to solemnize the ordinance as their brethren do in more favored lands, the native Saints would seldom, if ever, partake of the sacrament. **But in these strange conditions the Lord accepts instead of bread and wine, or bread and water, the meat of the coconut as the emblem of the body and its milk as the emblem of the blood of our crucified Lord.** This is the best the people there can do; therefore, it is accepted of God; but, if we, with our advantages, inspired by some whim or fanciful notion, were to make such changes, we would expose ourselves to the displeasures of the Lord, because we could present no justification for such a change. Any willful departure from that which the Lord has commanded is dangerous in the extreme. It is by such departures the Church of Christ has in past times left the true path; little by little they went astray. **The Lord accepts water at the sacrament instead of wine; when there is no bread, He accepts that which is used in its stead; but the ordinances of God's house cannot be deviated from."**

- Juvenile Instructor, September 1, 1897

In our day, the standard practice in the Church is to use bread and water for the sacrament emblems. Bread and water are substances that are usually readily available to the Saints scattered around the world as they hold their sacrament services. Exceptions and departures from this norm are now seldom necessary. **However, during the nearly 200-year history of the Church, things other than regular bread and water have sometimes been used as sacrament emblems.** Let's look at some historical information about the emblems of the sacrament.

- **It Mattereth Not** – In August 1830, the Prophet Joseph Smith was taught a lesson about sacrament emblems by a heavenly messenger. As recorded in the preface to Doctrine and Covenants 27, we read: "In preparation for a religious service at which the sacrament of bread and wine was to be administered, Joseph set out to procure wine for the occasion. He was met by a heavenly messenger and received this revelation:"

  - **Doctrine and Covenants 27:2-4 – "For behold, I say unto you, that it mattereth not what ye shall eat or what ye shall drink when ye partake of the sacrament, if it so be that ye do it with an eye single to my glory**…Wherefore, a commandment I give unto you, that you shall not purchase wine neither strong drink of your enemies; Wherefore, you shall partake of none except it is made new among you."

After receiving this information from the messenger, Joseph returned home and made home-made wine for the sacrament service.

- **The Sacrament as a Meal** – When Christ instituted the sacrament at the Last Supper, it was in the context of a meal. **In the early days of the restored Church, the sacrament was sometimes served as a meal – a ceremonial meal.**

  - Ugo A. Perego, in his essay *The Changing Forms of Latter-day Sacrament*, mentions that having the sacrament in the early years of the Church would sometimes include partaking of bread and wine in a quantity similar to a normal meal, **"to the filling both physically and spiritually of those in attendance."**

  - At times, the sacrament was administered by Joseph Smith during the School of the Prophets in Kirtland. (The School of the Prophets began in 1833 and continued for several years. Meetings were held in the room above Newell K. Whitney's store.) **Minutes from those meetings indicate that the sacrament followed "the ancient order," with bread broken into pieces as large as a fist and each person having their own cup.** Those attending the school partook of the elements of the sacrament as though they were eating a meal.

  - In a previously mentioned article, *The Lord's Supper in Early Mormonism*, Justin Bray recounts that in Painesville, Ohio in June of 1836, Joseph Smith provided the Lord's Supper to his mother, Lucy Mack Smith, his aunt, Clarissa, and others. He said Joseph followed "the ancient order" in administering the sacrament, with those who were

68

> partakers **eating and drinking until they satisfied their appetites.**
>
> o President George Q. Cannon, in the January 15, 1897 issue of the *Juvenile Instructor*, said that in the early days of the Church, "the bread and the wine were not passed as is the custom now among us. **It was an actual supper**…This would be the proper manner to administer this ordinance now if circumstances permitted."

- **Wine and Then Water** – Historical accounts indicate that wine was the common substance used for the sacrament during the early years of the Church. It appears that the first time water was used was in April 1837 during a solemn assembly in the Kirtland Temple. **After that, as the Church grew and expanded, water gradually began to be substituted for wine as circumstances dictated,** but wine was still the preferred choice with water being the exception. By early in the Utah era (from 1847 on), leaders moved more and more towards using water rather than wine for the sacrament. It wasn't until early in the 20th century, however, that water replaced wine throughout the Church as the official element for the sacrament.

- **Toquerville Mission** – An interesting bit of Church history involves the call of Brother John C. Naegle on a mission to Toquerville, Utah in 1866. **He was called by President Brigham Young to set up a wine mission for the Church.** Toquerville, located about 30 miles south of Cedar City, had the ideal soil and climate for growing fruit, especially grapes. Brother Naegle, a German immigrant and experienced vintner, moved to Toquerville and commenced to plant grapes, build a large rock house with a wine cellar, and make sacrament wine. At the height of the Toquerville wine mission, the winery produced 3,000 gallons of sacrament wine a year, much of which was shipped by wagon in 40-gallon casks to ZCMI in Salt Lake City, which then sold the wine to wards in the area. (Note – John C.

Naegle, whose old rock house still stands near the south end of Toquerville, was the great-great grandfather of one of my former bishops.)

- **Coconuts, Fresh Fruits, Dried Banana Chips, Crackers, Tortillas, Juices, Etc.** – As indicated previously, coconuts were sometimes used for the sacrament in the early days of the Church, with coconut meat representing the body of Christ and coconut milk the blood. Church records and the journals of members show us that, out of necessity, at certain times other items have also been used as sacrament emblems – **items such as fresh fruits, dried banana chips, crackers, tortillas, juices, etc.**

- **Latter-day Saint Servicemen and Servicewomen** – Military service brings unusual circumstances. **There have been a number of instances during times of war when Latter-day Saint servicemen and servicewomen were not able to use bread and water for the sacrament.** Instead, items such as pound cake, cookies, biscuits, fuel bars, and fruit beverages **that were provided in their military C-rations, K-rations, and MREs (Meals Ready to Eat)** were used. Because regular sacrament trays were often not available, it was sometimes necessary to use mess kits and canteen cups to serve the sacrament.

- **Latter-day Saint Members During and After Wartime** – Many stories have been told about how Church members during and after wartime have had to make substitutions for the normal sacrament emblems. For instance, Frederick W. Babbel in his interesting book *On Wings of Faith* writes about how he accompanied Elder Ezra Taft Benson as Elder Benson visited the Saints in Europe at the end of World War II to assess how they were getting along. Brother Babbel described attending a sacrament meeting in France where the members of the Church had no bread. **So, they retrieved potato peelings from the trash bins of the American troops stationed in their town and used those peelings as the emblems of the bread.** Elder Benson recounted this incident in his October 1980 General Conference talk when he said, "I cannot forget the French Saints who, unable to obtain bread, used potato peelings for the emblems of the sacrament."

- **Gluten Intolerance** – In recent years, a new Church policy has provided guidance to priesthood leaders and members concerning an important topic – that of gluten intolerance as it relates to the sacrament. This policy says that members who are gluten intolerant are encouraged to discuss the matter with a member of the bishopric to see what adaptations could be made to the sacrament. **Under this policy, members may provide allergen-free bread or another broken bread-like substitute in a sealed plastic bag or cup to the priesthood holders who prepare the sacrament.** This item can be placed on a separate tray or in a separate location on one of the regular bread trays. The bishopric then helps those who pass the sacrament know which members to pass the allergen-free sacrament emblem to.

Although there have been slight variations and adjustments in the sacrament over the years, **the purpose of the ordinance has remained fixed and constant.** Elder Jeffrey R. Holland, in a general conference talk in October 1995, spoke about the importance and sacred nature of the sacrament:

"With a crust of bread, always broken, blessed, and offered first, we remember His bruised body and broken heart, his physical suffering…With a small cup of water, we remember the shedding of Christ's blood and the depth of his spiritual suffering, anguish which began in the Garden of Gethsemane…The Savior's spiritual suffering and the shedding of his innocent blood, so lovingly and freely given, paid the debt (for our sins). **That is why every ordinance of the gospel focuses in one way or another on the Atonement of the Lord Jesus Christ, and surely that is why this particular ordinance with all its symbolism and imagery comes to us more readily and more repeatedly than any other in our life. It comes in what has been called the most sacred, the most holy, of all the meetings in the Church."**

Sacrament Term

Emblems

I like that we refer to the bread and water used in the sacrament ordinance as **the emblems of the sacrament,** and insofar as I can determine, we are unique among churches in doing so (with the exception of several offshoots of our church). Emblems, of course, are representative symbols. In the case of the sacrament, **the emblems symbolize and represent the Savior's body and blood, as well as all that He is and all that He means to us** – His exemplary life, His magnificent Atonement, and His crucifixion and resurrection in behalf of all mankind.

Our use of the word emblems is scriptural. Appearing only once in our standard works (in Doctrine and Covenants 20:40), its usage there is precise, stating clearly that the bread and water are the emblems of the flesh and blood of Christ.

We also find the word emblems in several of our sacrament hymns, such as *While of These Emblems We Partake*; *In Remembrance of Thy Suffering*; and *God, Our Father, Hear Us Pray*. **The sacrament emblems are most sacred and significant,** and I am humbled whenever I am privileged to partake of the emblems or to be involved in their preparation, blessing, or passing.

No Arms? No Problem!

Among my keepsakes is a personally autographed photo of a young man named Alex. Alex, who I have known for a number of years, wrote a message to me on the back of the photo:

"To Lee from Alex. Thank you for thinking of me and checking on me!! Alex."

On the front of the photo is a picture of Alex dressed in his Sunday best, ready to pass the sacrament. However, the message on the back of the photo is not in Alex's handwriting – **it is in Alex's footwriting.** You see, Alex was born with no arms and with just a single finger protruding out of his right shoulder.

Alex is a great inspiration to me and to his many friends and neighbors. Right from the time he came into this world, he set about to do everything with his feet that people his age did with their hands – like playing video games, participating in sports, riding all-terrain vehicles, and even swimming. **He learned how to write using a pen held between his toes, he developed the ability to dial a phone, and he even is able to play the guitar.**

As Alex grew up in the Church and approached Aaronic Priesthood age, those around him assumed he would receive the priesthood at the designated age but that he would not be able to pass the sacrament with the other deacons. After all, how can you hold a sacrament tray if you don't have arms? But his family, his bishop, his priesthood advisor – and especially Alex – weren't about to let that stop him. **Alex had spent his whole life figuring out how to do things that were normally off-limits to people with no arms, so why should this be any different?**

The solution was a custom-made plastic apparatus to carry the sacrament trays. With the support of Alex's bishop, his mother and priesthood advisor met with a designer at a plastic products company and decided that **what was needed was something that would hold onto Alex rather than something that Alex would hold onto.** Soon a type of platform was fabricated that consisted of a white-colored flat plastic surface trimmed with a two-inch plastic retaining strip. The device was large enough to hold either a standard-sized bread or water sacrament tray. The design included two nylon straps to secure the platform to Alex – one that went around Alex's waist and one that looped around his neck. Both straps were adjustable to make sure the apparatus fit tightly.

Alex was then able to take his place with the other deacons and pass the sacrament to the members of the

congregation using his specially made device. After the sacrament prayer, a priest would place one of the sacrament trays on Alex's platform. Alex would then go from row to row in his assigned area and present the tray to those in attendance. (Note - When it was time for him to partake of his own bread and water, a deacon standing next to Alex would assist him.)

As you can imagine, seeing Alex pass the sacrament helped make the sacrament ordinance even more special for those in the meeting. Alex's advisor, Brother Hopkin, said, **"Alex is an inspiration to me personally. He could have taken the easy way out and declined to do his priesthood duty, but that is not Alex's way. Alex does all he possibly can by himself and loves participating in the responsibilities of the Aaronic Priesthood."** Alex's bishop, Bishop Francom, said, **"If a 12-year-old boy without arms can pass the sacrament, I can do anything in the Church."**

After I became acquainted with Alex, I invited him to join me as I spoke to a youth group about the history of the sacrament. As part of the presentation, I asked Alex to put on his special device and express his feelings about the ordinance. As he told those in attendance his story and talked about the many things he had learned to do without hands, **he made special mention of the sacred nature of the sacrament and how important it is for us to appreciate the ordinance and be grateful for the Savior and His Atonement as we partake of the sacrament.**

Alex is now past Aaronic Priesthood age and he has been kind enough to provide me with another meaningful keepsake. He has given me custody of his special plastic apparatus and has given me approval to continue showing it during my Church presentations. **He hopes his device and his story will be inspirational to others, especially to those who may be feeling sorry for themselves because of some physical limitation or handicap.**

Opportunities to Participate and Serve

Now, just a note about the role of members of the Church who may have special needs or who are handicapped in some manner. **President Russell M. Nelson has repeatedly stressed how we all are God's children, how each person is important, and how God loves all of us.** He, as well as other leaders, have taught us that **members with disabilities can serve in almost any Church assignment.** They have counseled us that as we prayerfully consider each person's abilities and desires, we will be inspired to provide them with appropriate opportunities to participate and serve. The *General Handbook* says, **"Church members are encouraged to follow the Savior's example of offering hope, understanding, and love to those who have disabilities. As teachers and leaders, you have the opportunity to assist all members of your ward, including those with disabilities, to return to the presence of our Heavenly Father."** (*General Handbook* 38.8.31)

I am grateful for people such as Alex who inspire and bless us with their service and who often do so while facing significant personal challenges.

(Note – For an additional account of how a special young man with challenges fulfilled his Aaronic Priesthood responsibilities, I recommend you read or watch President Steven J. Lund's October 2020 general conference address titled *Finding Joy in Christ*. In his talk, President Lund (the Church's Young Men General President) touchingly tells about his grandson, Tanner, who insisted on going to church to pass the sacrament despite suffering greatly from being in the advanced stages of cancer.)

Sacrament Term

Sanctuary

A sanctuary is the most sacred and holy place within a church. In our Latter-day Saint meetinghouses, **our sanctuary would be the chapel.** In the buildings of other religions, the sanctuary typically refers to the area around the altar.

The Church of Jesus Christ of Latter-day Saints uses terminology that differs from that used in other faiths when referring to our houses of worship. We refer to the buildings we meet in on Sunday as meetinghouses, churches, wards, and stake centers. Inside our buildings, we have chapels, sacrament tables, cultural halls, classrooms, baptismal fonts, media centers, serving areas, and bishop's offices. In the buildings of other faiths, they have sanctuaries, altars, chancels, apses, naves, transepts, and confessionals.

(Note – In the churches of other religions, the sanctuary is often located in the eastern part of the building – the direction of the resurrection.)

The Flame Flickered and Dimmed

In speaking of the state of the Church of Christ after the crucifixion of the Savior, Elder Boyd K. Packer likened what happened to a candle whose **flame flickered and dimmed.** He said:

"Despite opposition, the Twelve established the Church of Jesus Christ; and despite persecution, it flourished. But as the centuries passed, **the flame flickered and dimmed. Ordinances were changed or abandoned.** The line was broken, and the authority to confer the Holy Ghost as a gift was gone. **The Dark Ages of apostasy settled over the world.**" (April 2000 general conference address.)

While the sacrament was not abandoned during this time, **it was one of the sacred ordinances in the Church of Christ that was affected during the long period of time between the death of the Savior and the restoration of the gospel.** The changes in the sacrament were the result of several factors, including:

Authority Was Lost

Priesthood, the power and authority of God, is essential in performing the ordinances of the gospel. As had been prophesied, after the time of Christ the apostles and prophets were persecuted and martyred, resulting in the priesthood eventually being taken from the earth. **The absence of proper authority left a void** that could not be filled until the priesthood was restored to Joseph Smith by heavenly messengers. Without the guidance of true apostles and prophets, a great diversity of churches arose during the long period of darkness, churches that had a form of godliness but who denied the power thereof (see Joseph Smith History 1:19). **And those many churches developed a great diversity of opinions and practices concerning the sacrament.**

Simplicity Was Lost

The sacrament was a simple ordinance when Christ introduced it at the Last Supper. During the centuries when the true Church of Christ was not on the earth, the simplicity of the sacrament was often replaced by complex ceremonies, many of which were influenced by pagan philosophy. In many cases, these elaborate rules and rituals took away from the spirit and purpose of the ordinance, causing worshipers to lose sight of its true meaning and beauty. As written by Elder James E. Talmage in chapter eight of *The Great Apostasy*:

> **"The sacrament, as instituted by the Savior and as administered during the days of the apostolic ministry, was as simple as it was sacred and solemn**…As soon as the power of the priesthood departed, much disputation arose in matters of the ordinance, and the observance of the sacrament became distorted. **Theological teachers strove to foster the idea that there was much mystery attending this naturally simple and most impressive ordinance."**

Doctrine Was Distorted

As many plain and precious truths of the gospel were lost (see 1 Nephi 13:26), some of the doctrine pertaining to the Lord's Supper became distorted and altered. Without revelation, people relied on human wisdom, **resulting in false ideas being introduced into the teachings about the sacrament.**

Examples of Sacrament Practices

Following are some of the practices and ideas about the sacrament ordinance **that exist in many of today's churches,** as compared to those of The Church of Jesus Christ of Latter-day Saints. (Please note that although our Church calls the ordinance "the sacrament," many of today's faiths use other terminology when referring to it – such as "the Last Supper," "the Lord's Supper," "Holy Communion," the "Eucharist," etc. For simplicity, I have called it "the sacrament" in most of the following examples.)

- Several churches teach that the act of partaking of the sacrament **provides forgiveness of sin.** We do not believe that our sins are forgiven as we partake of the sacrament.

- A number of churches **direct their sacrament prayers to Jesus Christ** rather than to Heavenly Father. We direct our sacrament prayers, to "O God, the Eternal Father…"

- Calling it "the Lord's Evening Meal," one faith's communion service **is always held after sundown.** We believe it doesn't matter what time of day we hold sacrament services.

- Some faiths believe that the bread and water are **transformed into the actual body and blood of Jesus Christ** during the sacrament. We do not believe the elements of the sacrament undergo such a transformation. (Please see the term "transubstantiation" at the end of Chapter 20.)

- One Christian church **does not practice the sacrament at all.** They do not feel the sacrament is necessary in order to live a proper Christian life. As followers of Jesus Christ, we believe that partaking of the sacrament on a regular basis is important.

- Several churches don't have the sacrament because they believe it places **too much emphasis on an outward ritual** that takes away from an inward spiritual devotion to the Savior. We believe that the sacrament improves our inward spiritual devotion to the Savior.

- Some churches teach that partaking of the sacrament **guarantees the recipient will have eternal life.** We do not believe eternal life comes solely by way of partaking of the sacrament.

- One group of churches hands out plates of broken bread and small cups of juice to all those in the congregation. Holding both elements of the sacrament in their hands until everyone has been served, **they then all consume the bread and liquid in unison.** We do not believe the elements of the sacrament have to be consumed in unison.

- Some faiths follow the practice of **dipping the wafer (or bread) into the cup of wine (or water) and then eating the moistened wafer.** We believe in partaking of the bread first and then the water. (Please see the term "intinction" at the end of Chapter 24.)

- Many faiths have developed **very formal and ritualistic sacrament proceedings** that often include lengthy prayers, rites, readings, and litanies. Our sacrament prayers are brief and the administration of our sacrament is done in a simple and unpretentious manner.

- Many faiths have **specific rules and instructions concerning the type of wafer (or bread) and wine (or water)** that are used in their sacrament services. The standard practice in our Church today is to use regular bread and water, when available.

- Various denominations differ about having what is called **"closed" versus "open" communion.** Some restrict the sacrament just to members of their faith. Others allow all in attendance to partake. Still others permit only those in good standing who have recently confessed their sins to participate. Our Church's policy is that, although the sacrament is meant primarily for members of the Church, nothing should be done to prevent others from partaking of it.

- In order to partake of the sacrament, the members of one denomination **must be at peace with all others and must have made a recent confession to their priest.** In our Church, we do not believe that these are prerequisites for partaking of the sacrament.

- In one particular denomination, those who come forward to stand in the communion line may choose to either receive the sacrament or receive a blessing. **If they want a blessing rather than the sacrament, they cross their arms over their chest as a sign to the priest.** The priest then blesses them as they come through the line but does not offer them the sacrament. In our Church, we provide priesthood blessings separately from the sacrament.

- One Christian denomination considers **every meal they eat each day to be a Eucharistic feast,** so they do not observe the sacrament in their meetings. We do not consider our normal meals to be a replacement for the sacrament.

- Several groups of churches **link the sacrament to fasting.** In these churches, members may not partake of the sacrament unless they have fasted from all food and water from midnight the night before until they partake of the sacrament. In our Church, many members do fast once each month on what is called Fast Sunday, but fasting is not a requirement on that Sunday or any other Sunday in order to partake of the sacrament.

- In preparation for the sacrament, members of some faiths participate in various **pre-communion prayers and rituals.** We do not have such pre-sacrament requirements.

Conclusion

After many centuries without the fulness of the gospel, Christ's ancient church was restored along with the true principles and practices of the sacrament. **I am grateful that the flame that flickered and dimmed for so many years, as mentioned in Elder Packer's talk, is again burning brightly.** What a blessing that is!

Hark, All Ye Nations!
Hymn No. 264

Verse No. 2

Searching in darkness, nations have wept;
Watching for dawn, their vigil they've kept.
All now rejoice, the long night is o'er;
Truth is on earth once more!

Chorus

Oh, how glorious from the throne above,
Shines the gospel light of truth and love!
Bright as the sun, this heavenly ray,
Lights ev'ry land today.

Sacrament Term

Da Vinci's The Last Supper

Leonardo Da Vinci's *The Last Supper* is one of the world's most famous and beloved paintings. An interesting aspect of the painting is Da Vinci's choice of which precise moment during the Last Supper to depict Christ and his apostles. Rather than choose the time when Jesus was blessing and passing the sacrament, **Da Vinci selected the moment right after Christ's announcement that one of the apostles will betray Him.**

The painting vividly shows the shocked and concerned faces of the apostles and the emotions that Christ's declaration generates in them. *The Last Supper* is a late 15th century mural painting that is located in the refectory of the Convent of Santa Maria della Grazie in Milan, Italy.

20-mm Shell Casings

Permission to meet had already been obtained from Church leaders in Salt Lake City, but the aircraft carrier's rules said that one of the two chaplains on board the ship – either the Catholic chaplain or the Protestant chaplain – had to also give permission for the group of Latter-day Saint sailors to meet each Sunday in a worship service. **Ralph Albiston, a member of the Church who was born in Hawkins Basin, Idaho,** had already talked to the Catholic chaplain, and had been refused permission. As Ralph then asked the Protestant chaplain, **Chaplain Safford,** if he would allow the services to take place, the chaplain hesitated and then said he would grant the okay with one stipulation. **The stipulation was that he, the chaplain, would have to be present at all the meetings.**

Ralph Albiston, and the 23 other Latter-day Saint sailors on board the **USS Intrepid aircraft carrier,** were elated and began meeting each Sunday in the ship's chapel for a worship service that included the sacrament. **At each meeting, sitting quietly in the corner, sat Chaplain Safford.**

The year was 1944, and the Intrepid was heavily involved in World War II. The ship was a fully armed aircraft carrier equipped with approximately 100 aircraft and with a complement of 3,000 officers and enlisted men on board. Besides the planes, the ship had an arsenal of weapons consisting of a number of 127-

millimeter cannons, an array of 40-mm guns, and 46 anti-aircraft 20-mm guns.

As the group of sailors partook of the sacrament each Sunday, Ralph felt that they needed a more proper means to pass the water for the sacrament, **so he went to the flight deck gun tubs and found empty 20-millimeter shell casings** that had been expended in shooting at enemy aircraft. He picked up about 40 of the casings and took them to the machine shop on board the ship. There he had them cut to the length he specified, a length of about two inches, so they could hold the proper amount of water and serve as **individual water cups** for the sacrament.

He then gave each of the member sailors several of the shells and asked them to clean and polish them, which was a difficult process. Each sailor worked hard at the task, and soon the shells came back ready to be used for the sacrament. During its tour of duty, the Intrepid sustained some damage during a battle in the war and was sent to San Francisco for repairs. **On the way, it stopped in Honolulu, where Ralph took the cleaned-up shell bottoms to a shop to have them silver plated.** After the repairs to the ship had been completed in San Francisco, the Intrepid returned to the Pacific war area, stopping briefly in Hawaii, where Ralph picked up the newly plated sacrament cups.

A beautiful wooden tray with a handle on each end was made by one of the other sailors on board the ship to hold 20 cups. **This special wartime sacrament tray, which added greatly to their weekly sacrament service, was used for about 18 months by the sailors on the Intrepid until the war ended.**

Other Military Sacrament Experiences

Most Latter-day Saint servicemen and servicewomen, especially during wartime, value their Church membership, look forward to worship services, **and long for the sacrament.** There are many touching stories, similar to the one just related, that talk about the interesting and unusual things that devoted members of the armed services have done so they can attend church and partake of the sacrament while serving their country. In fact, there are books on the subject, including the excellent *Saints at War* by Robert C. Freeman and Dennis A. Wright. Among the stories they relate in their book, are:

- **Lloyd Miller**, a marine serving in New Caledonia circa 1942 wrote: "We would hold our own sacrament meeting together away from the rest of the people. We sat down on a big fallen log where it was quiet. We had a discussion on religion as well as having the sacrament. **We felt the spirit very strongly.**" (page 361)

- **Robert L. Backman** (a future general authority) writes about Easter morning 1945 while serving in the 43rd Division of the Army: "I will never forget, as we partook of the sacrament, **the priests knelt at the table and could not get through the prayers because they were so emotional about it.** I watched some of the men who acted as deacons, tears coursing down their cheeks as they passed the sacrament in our mess gear to the congregation – and those receiving it feeling the same spirit, tears in their eyes." (pages 250-251)

- **Louis Fife**, in the 382nd Infantry Regiment in Okinawa in 1945: "During a Sunday at the front, we dug a large foxhole and rounded up all the LDS guys to hold a meeting. There were about five or six of us there. We had a very inspirational meeting. We tried to remember the sacrament prayers, but didn't get them exactly right. **Though muddy and in a foxhole, the Spirit was there more than in any other place, other than the temple, that I have ever experienced.**" (page 317)

- **J. Heber Moulton**, quartermaster, 6th Infantry Division, New Guinea and Luzon: "I became acquainted with a Sergeant Johnson. One Sunday morning I asked him to go to church with me. When I blessed the sacrament, as sometimes happens, a quiet peaceful feeling came over me. After church, Johnson was really anxious to get me alone. He was a big man. He grabbed me by the shoulder and said, **'Moulton, where did you get that prayer? You didn't**

make it up.' I tried to explain how we got the prayer and what it means to us. Seldom do I hear the prayer, but what I think of Sergeant Johnson." (page 366)

The Intrepid Sacrament Tray

A few years ago, as I read in the *Church News* the story about the 20-mm shell casings being used on the USS Intrepid as sacrament cups, I became aware that the water tray they made on that ship had been donated to the Church. After some phone calls, I was able to talk to Alan Morrell, an artifact curator at the Church History Museum in Salt Lake City, and he confirmed that the Church did have the tray as well as other old sacrament memorabilia. Alan was kind enough to invite my wife, Holly, and me to come see these items, so one day we drove downtown to the museum to meet with Brother Morrell. The tray was in the climate-controlled basement storage area of the museum. **After we donned rubber gloves, Alan led us to a cabinet where the tray was located.** He brought it out, removed the protective cloth from around it, and gave us a chance to hold it and photograph it.

I explained to Brother Morrell about the firesides and talks that I give concerning the history of the sacrament and asked if I could borrow the tray and the cups to use in my presentations. He smiled, and then kindly explained that that would not be possible.

Well, I had seen the tray and had a photo of it, **so I went home and proceeded to make a duplicate copy of that tray and its cups.** The wood part and the handles were not too difficult, but finding some 20-mm shell casings was the challenge. I called all over town and searched high and low without success. It then crossed my mind to check with the big Army surplus store located on the west side of the I-15 freeway north of Ogden. In huge letters on the front of the building I had often seen their sign that says, **"We've got anything you want…if we can find it."**

I phoned the store, and was transferred to the manager of one of the departments. I explained what I was looking for and what the purpose was for the shell casings (which he kind of understood because he was a member of the Church). He said that they had that type of shell casings – but he had no idea where they were. I thanked him and asked him to please call me if he found them. Later that day, the phone rang and the man told me he had located them. **I drove to the store and bought enough to fill the tray – plus a few extras.**

Then, with the help of another friend of mine named Randy (a different Randy than the one in Chapter 7), I cut the casings down to size, cleaned them up, and had a small metal plating company in town metal plate them for me. (When I explained to the metal plating man, who was not a member, what the purpose of the shells was, he got really confused and gave me a funny look.) The shells turned out great, looking just like the ones in the museum, **so I now have an almost-identical copy of the Intrepid tray and its sacrament water cups.** It is one of my favorite pieces of sacrament memorabilia.

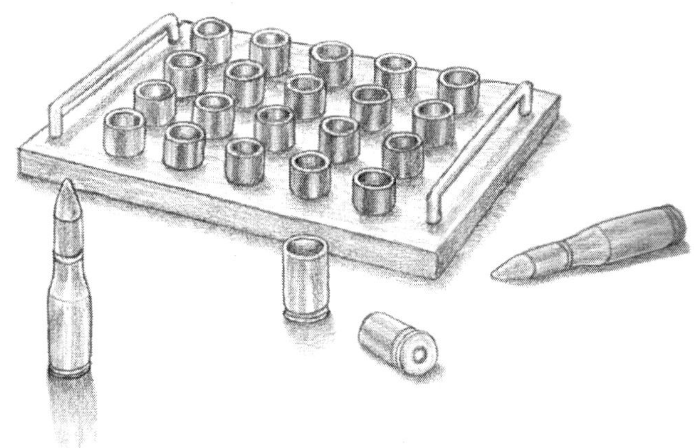

Sacrament Stories

I love hearing stories about the sacrament. **I have found over and over again that the sacrament holds a very special place in the hearts of Church members.** We love the sacrament and enjoy relating experiences to each other about the times we have been privileged to partake of it, often in unusual places and in interesting ways. We look forward to it each week and miss the sacrament greatly when we aren't able to have it. I am grateful for this sacred ordinance and express my appreciation to Heavenly Father and his son Jesus Christ for making it possible for me to have the opportunity of receiving the sacrament on a regular basis.

****

Additional Information About the USS Intrepid Aircraft Carrier and its Latter-day Saint Crew

- The ship was first commissioned in 1943 and decommissioned for the last time in 1974.
- It saw action during World War II and the Vietnam War.
- It has an overall length of 874 feet, nearly the length of three football fields.
- Its top speed is 33 knots (38 mph), which is very fast for such a large ship. The fastest cruise ships travel at about 30 knots.
- During World War II, it was torpedoed once. It also was hit by four separate Japanese kamikaze aircraft during the war.
- It once served as a space capsule recovery ship for the Mercury and Gemini space missions.
- It is now a museum in New York harbor. Called the Intrepid Sea, Air & Space Museum, it is docked in the Hudson River at Pier 86 on the west side of Manhattan. Besides the aircraft carrier, the museum has a full-size submarine, a Concord SST, the space shuttle Enterprise, and other aircraft and military items.
- In 2001 after the 9/11 bombings, the FBI set up their temporary field headquarters on the USS Intrepid as they investigated the terrorist attacks.
- This is the first aircraft carrier and fourth US Navy ship to bear the name Intrepid. Intrepid means resolute, dauntless, and fearless.

- Intrepid was also the name of the Lunar Module on Apollo 12.
- We know the names of 13 of the Latter-day Saint sailors who were part of the sacrament tray story. Alphabetically, they are: Ralph Albiston, Burt Tracy Anderson, Clyde Brown, Ray Campanga, Dick Larsen, Bill Larson, Dee Orr, Lane Peterson, Lloyd Richins, Art Sadler, Dean Salvison, Lynn Shearer, and Reed Woolf.
- **Concerning Chaplain Safford, I'm sad to say that I have no information about what became of him,** but trust that he benefitted from listening in on the meetings on board the ship. (Wouldn't it be a great addition to the story if he had been converted because of his experience attending the sacrament meetings?)

Sacrament Term

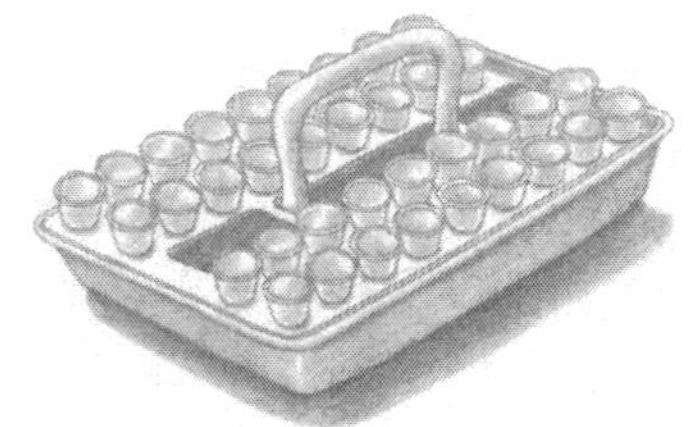

Unleavened Bread

In cooking, a leaven or raising agent is a substance used to lighten or soften the dough or batter. Leavens, such as baker's yeast, cause a foaming action that, over time, infuses gas bubbles into the mixture. The gas bubbles consist largely of carbon dioxide. Unleavened bread is any of a variety of breads which do not contain a raising agent.

When Christ celebrated the Last Supper prior to His crucifixion, the bread He broke and gave to His apostles in remembrance of His body was unleavened bread. This was in keeping with the Jewish Passover tradition which forbade the use of any foods containing leaven during the Passover period. The Passover commemorated Israel's deliverance from Egyptian bondage. When the children of Israel left Egypt, they did so in haste. **They did not have time for bread to rise, so it was made on that very first Passover without leaven.** In subsequent Passover celebrations, unleavened bread has been symbolic of Israel's rapid flight from Egypt. (See Exodus 12:12-20 and Deuteronomy 16:8.)

Unleavened breads are generally flat breads, but not all flat breads are unleavened. Unleavened breads can be found in kitchens, markets, and restaurants all around the world, such as those in Israel (matzo), Mexico (tortillas), Ethiopia (kitcha), India (roti and chapati), Finland (rieska), British Isles (bannock), Colombia and Venezuela (arepa), and Arabia (arboud).

Sacrament Gems in Sunday School

Although I was too young to remember doing so, **my parents told me that my first talk from a church pulpit was when I gave the sacrament gem in Junior Sunday School.** That event took place somewhere around 1950 when I was three or four years old. Our ward, the Stratford Ward, had both a Senior Sunday School and a Junior Sunday School. **Each group met separately for opening exercises** – the adults in the chapel upstairs and the children at the same time downstairs in the Relief Society room. (The Relief Society room was a carpeted room with a small pulpit and a **sacrament table**. During the week, it was where the Relief Society held its regular weekday meeting.) On Sunday morning, after each of the opening exercises concluded, the children and adults would "separate for classes."

Sunday meeting schedules in the Church were quite different back then. Our ward's weekly priesthood meeting was held on Sunday morning. The adult men and Aaronic Priesthood boys would go to the meetinghouse early for priesthood meeting, which consisted of opening exercises followed by separation into quorums for a lesson. After priesthood meeting, they would go home to pick up their families and return for Sunday School, which was held later in the morning. After Sunday School concluded, we would travel home for lunch and Sabbath afternoon activities before returning to the meetinghouse in the evening for sacrament meeting. **In my ward, we partook of the sacrament twice each Sunday – in Sunday School in the morning and in sacrament meeting in the evening.**

Sacrament Gems

Sacrament gems were short thoughts about the Savior and the sacrament that were taken from the scriptures or the hymn book. During Sunday School opening exercises, the assigned person would stand at the pulpit prior to the blessing of the sacrament and recite the sacrament gem. The members of the congregation would repeat back the gem in unison. The sacrament would then be blessed and passed.

Here are several examples of sacrament gems that were used in the Sunday Schools of the Church:

"While of these emblems we partake
In Jesus' name and for His sake,
Let us remember and be sure
Our hearts and hands are clean and pure."
- For January 1910 (This was the Church's first sacrament gem.)

"The bread and water represent
His sacrifice for sin;
Ye Saints, partake and testify
You do remember Him."
- For October 1921

"And that thou mayest more fully keep thyself unspotted from the world, thou shalt go to the house of prayer and offer up thy sacraments upon my holy day."
- For March 1934

"And if ye do always remember me, ye shall have my Spirit to be with you."
- For Senior Sunday School in April 1973

"Jesus said: I am the resurrection, and the life."
- For Junior Sunday School in April 1973

Sacrament gems were a part of the Church for 70 years. Introduced in 1910, they were discontinued in 1980 when the consolidated three-hour block of meetings was instituted and Sunday School as a separate meeting was eliminated. When I mention sacrament gems to my grandchildren, they don't know what I'm talking about because they never experienced them. They also have never experienced having the sacrament twice each Sunday as I did. Since 1980, we have partaken of the sacrament only once each Sunday and since that time sacrament gems have not been part of Sunday School.

The History of Sunday School and the Sacrament

The history of the Sunday School as it relates to the sacrament in the Church is interesting. **The first formal Sunday School in the Church was held on December 9, 1849** in Salt Lake City under the direction of Richard Ballantyne, a Scottish convert who was acting on his own accord and not under the direction of the Church. He was concerned that young people were not always being taught the gospel in an effective manner, so he set up a school on Sunday mornings in his home to educate children in the principles of the gospel and the scriptures. The school proved successful and before long it was moved to his ward's meetinghouse.

The idea gained acceptance and soon others in the Salt Lake area were following Brother Ballantyne's pattern. Each school functioned independently. Seeing the value of the schools and realizing the benefits of a central organization, **Church leaders united the schools into one group on November 11, 1867.** Elder George Q. Cannon of the Quorum of the Twelve Apostles was made the head of the organization. His title was **general superintendent** and the organization was called **the Deseret Sunday School Union.**

(Note - A year before the Deseret Sunday School Union was formed, Elder Cannon had begun publishing a magazine called the *Juvenile Instructor.* He owned the publication. This periodical was the primary method of communicating lessons, teaching methods, and procedures to the various Sunday Schools. After becoming the head of the Deseret Sunday School Union in 1867, the Church asked Elder Cannon to continue publishing the magazine and Elder Cannon continued to own it.)

Then a major change in the Church's policy concerning the sacrament took place, a change that would last for 103 years until the consolidated schedule was introduced. **Bishops and their counselors were instructed by the First Presidency in 1877 to begin attending the weekly Sunday School meetings in their ward (which they had not been doing on a regular basis) and to administer the sacrament in each Sunday School meeting.** Thus, in addition to partaking of the sacrament in the weekly sacrament meeting, those who attended Sunday School also had the sacrament during that meeting. To help the various wards and branches know how to properly administer the sacrament in Sunday School, policies and procedures concerning the sacrament service were commonly communicated to the general Church in the *Juvenile Instructor*. **Eventually, in 1901, the Church purchased the *Juvenile Instructor* magazine from the Cannon family.** In 1929, the name of the magazine was changed to the ***Instructor*** and in 1970 the magazine was replaced by the ***New Era.***

On pages 9 and 10 of the January 1910 issue of the *Juvenile Instructor*, the general Sunday School superintendency of the Church issued the following directive:

> "Some time ago a resolution was passed by the General Board recommending to the schools that immediately prior to the administration of the sacrament the school recite in concert a short appropriate verse or text designed to concentrate the minds of the children upon the sacred ordinances to be administered…We have thought it wise to adopt the plan of recommending through the columns of the *Juvenile* each month a sacrament gem to be used by all of the schools of the Church during that month, this gem to be learned thoroughly by the people and recited in concert immediately preceding the administration of the sacrament."

Thus, the sacrament gem was born. To create uniformity throughout the Church, each month the *Juvenile Instructor,* in a section called the Superintendents' Department, would announce the sacrament gem to be used in the upcoming month or months. A short line of prelude and postlude music to accompany the gem was often included in the instructions. A class in each ward was given the responsibility for the sacrament gem for the month, with the teacher selecting a student each week to recite the gem in front of the congregation. Sunday Schools grew in size as more youth and adults attended, so many wards added a separate Junior Sunday School meeting during the same time as Senior Sunday School. To take into account the more limited abilities of the younger children, **a shorter separate sacrament gem for the Junior Sunday School was instituted.**

President Russell M. Nelson and Sunday School

Now, just a mention of the important role that **President Russell M. Nelson** played in the history of the Sunday School. In 1971, Russell M. Nelson, while serving as the president of the Bonneville Stake in Salt Lake City, was called to become the general superintendent of the Deseret Sunday School Union. This was his first general calling in the Church.

As we know, President Nelson is a very progressive leader who is not afraid to institute change. During his term of service, he met regularly with President Harold B. Lee, the president of the Church. In one of their meetings, **Superintendent Nelson suggested to President Lee that perhaps the time had come to remove the word "Union" from the name of the organization.** President Lee readily agreed and soon the named was changed to the **Deseret Sunday School.** This remained the name until 1980 when the consolidated meeting schedule was introduced and the word "Deseret" was dropped.

About a year after the organization's name was shortened, Superintendent Nelson pointed out to President Lee that the presiding authorities in priesthood quorums, the Relief Society, the Primary, and the Young Women's Mutual Improvement Association were called "presidents" and that they had "counselors." **However, in the Sunday School and the Young Men's Mutual Improvement Association, the leaders were**

called "superintendents" and they had "assistant superintendents" serving with them. Superintendent Nelson recommended to President Lee that a change be made, and within a short time, superintendents became presidents.

Other noteworthy changes and improvements that took place during President Nelson's eight-year term included the creation of centralized and coordinated curriculum, the introduction of a cycle of scripture instruction for adult classes, and the move to have communications and directions to the Sunday School take place through priesthood channels.

A Great Influence in My Life

As I look back on my life, **I am grateful for the influence the Sunday School has had on me.** A great deal of my understanding of the scriptures and the gospel plan has come by way of Sunday School lessons. I appreciate my Sunday School teachers. I am grateful that they were prayerful and conscientious in preparing and presenting their lessons each Sunday. **I loved the sacrament gems and am thankful that from time to time I was chosen to present them in Sunday School opening exercises.** Those inspirational thoughts were of great help to me in my efforts to focus on the Savior and His Atonement during the special times when I partook of the bread and water in remembrance of Him.

(Note – As I was doing research for this chapter, I discovered something I hadn't heard of before. Although it lasted for only a short period of time, the Church once instituted an organization called the **Deseret Sunday School Musical Union.** It had its own brass band with Charles J. Thomas as the conductor, it published its own *Union Music Book,* and it held annual musical festivals in the Tabernacle beginning in 1874.)

Sacrament Term

Winepress

In Biblical times, a winepress was a large basin, often cut out of limestone, that was used in the making of wine. Bunches of grapes would be placed in the basin and then several workers at a time would walk (tread) on the grapes in their bare feet (after having washed their feet thoroughly) to squeeze out the juice. The juice would then run down channels cut into the stone to be collected in jars. After cleaning and filtration, the juice would be aged and made into wine.

When referring to Jesus Christ's Atonement and that he overcame the world, the scriptures tell us that the Savior had **"trodden the winepress alone."** This is significant. It helps emphasize that the Savior by Himself – **alone and without the help of others** – took upon Him the sins of the world and enabled all to receive the gift of eternal life.

- **"I have trodden the winepress alone;** and of the people there was none with me." – Isaiah 63:3
- "When he shall deliver up the kingdom, and present it unto the Father, spotless, saying: **I have overcome and have trodden the winepress alone."** – Doctrine and Covenants 76:107
- "It is finished; it is finished! **The Lamb of God hath overcome and trodden the winepress alone."** – Doctrine and Covenants 88:106

In the April 2009 general conference, Elder Jeffrey R. Holland referred to this when he said, "I speak of the Savior's solitary task of shouldering alone the burden of our salvation. **Rightly He would say: 'I have trodden the winepress alone.'"**

Worthy to Perform, Worthy to Partake

Recently, an assistant temple matron speaking in our stake conference told a touching story about a man's desire to be found worthy when he passed from this life. After an illness, the man had died. The times for the viewing and funeral had been set, but the man's wife was a few minutes late arriving at the viewing. **When she finally came, she quietly entered the viewing room, walked to the casket, and slipped something into the shirt pocket of her husband who was lying in repose in the casket.**

When one of her friends asked her what she had placed in his pocket, she said that she put his temple recommend in it. **Before he died, she explained, he had asked her to make sure that his temple recommend was in his shirt pocket when he was buried so that there would be no question about his worthiness as he passed to the other side.** Having forgotten his request as she hurried to the viewing, his wish came to her mind as she approached the meetinghouse. Even though it would make her a little late, she returned to their home to get his recommend so it could be in his pocket as he was buried.

Worthiness is an important factor as we journey through life and participate in the Church. We need to be worthy to receive baptism, be given a calling, receive the priesthood, go on a mission, or enter the temple. Although it doesn't require temple worthiness, we also need to be worthy as it relates to the sacrament. **Those holding the priesthood who participate in the sacred ordinance need to be worthy to perform their duties, and those in the congregation who receive the sacrament, need to be worthy to partake of the emblems.**

Pertaining to sacrament worthiness, there are four places in the scriptures that talk about this:

- **I Corinthians 11:27-30** – "Wherefore whosoever shall eat this bread, and drink this cup of the Lord, unworthily, shall be guilty of the body and blood of the Lord…For he that eateth and drinketh unworthily, eateth and drinketh damnation to himself, not discerning the Lord's body. For this cause many are weak and sickly among you, and many sleep."
- **3 Nephi 18:28-29** – "And now behold, this is the commandment which I give unto you, that ye shall not suffer any one knowingly to partake of my flesh and blood unworthily, when ye shall administer it; For whoso eateth and drinketh my flesh and blood unworthily eateth and drinketh damnation to his soul; therefore if ye know that a man is unworthy to eat and drink of my flesh and blood ye shall forbid him."
- **4 Nephi 1:27** – "…yea, there were many churches which professed to know the Christ, and yet did deny the more parts of the gospel…and did administer that which was sacred unto him to whom it had been forbidden because of unworthiness."
- **Mormon 9:29** – "See that ye are not baptized unworthily; see that ye partake not of the sacrament of Christ unworthily; but see that ye do all things in worthiness…"

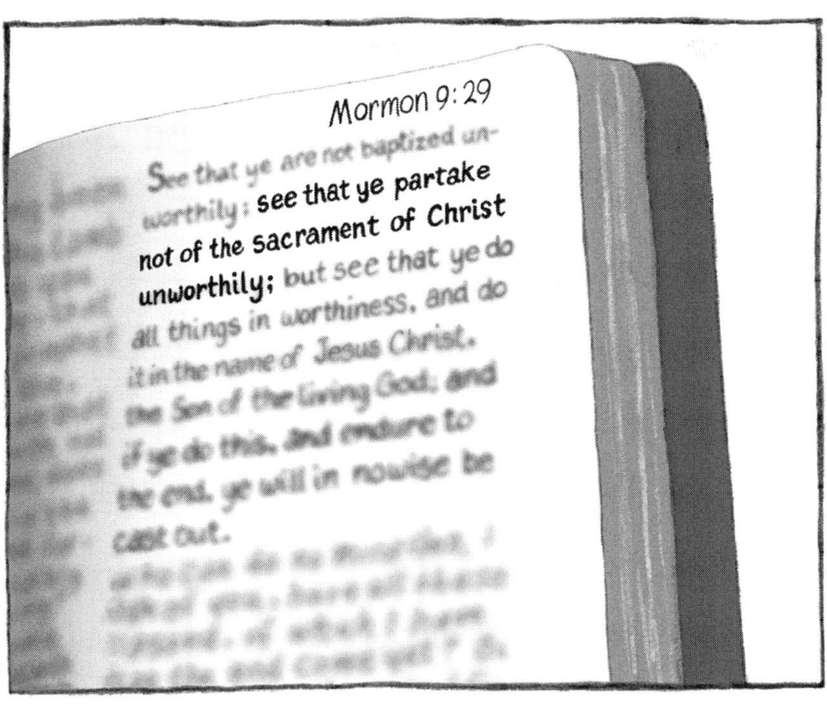

Throughout the history of the Church, worthiness when partaking of the sacrament or when performing sacrament duties has always been very important. Here are some examples of how this was viewed in the earlier days of the Church:

- **Let Trespassers Not Partake** – On March 8, 1831, less than a year after the organization of the Church, the Prophet Joseph Smith received direction from the Lord concerning Church services and the sacrament, as recorded in Doctrine and Covenants Section 46. The introduction to this section says, "In this early time of the Church, there had not yet developed a uniform pattern for the conducting of Church services. However, a custom of admitting only members and earnest investigators to the sacrament meetings and other assemblies of the Church had become somewhat general. This revelation expresses the will of the Lord relative to governing and conducting meetings." In verses 3 and 4, we read: "Nevertheless ye are commanded never to cast any one out of your public meetings, which are held before the world. **Ye are also commanded not to cast any one who belongeth to the church out of your sacrament meetings; nevertheless, if any have trespassed, let him not partake until he makes reconciliation.**"

- **Joseph Smith's Warning** – In February 1835, Joseph Smith issued a warning to Church members concerning participating unworthily in the sacrament. As recorded in Volume 2, Page 408 of the *History of the Church*, he said: "Previous to the administration, I spoke of the propriety of this institution (the sacrament) in the Church, **and urged the importance of doing it with acceptance before the Lord,** and asked, 'How long do you suppose a man may partake of this ordinance unworthily, and the Lord not withdraw His Spirit from him?'"

- **Withholding the Sacrament** – At times, the sacrament was withheld from congregations for short periods because of contention and division within the Church. This was particularly the case in 1856 and 1857. In an effort to help Church members take their religion more seriously and to put away their sins and transgressions, **the sacrament was omitted from some meetings for some time, even up to a few months.** Also during this time, known in Church history as the reformation period, some members were rebaptized to show their recommitment to the gospel.

- **Token of the New Covenant** – Elder George Reynolds, one of the presidents of the Seventy, in February 1895 said, "The sacrament is a token of the new covenant, and any who understands it will scarcely partake unless they are in fellowship in that covenant."

In today's Church, sincere members may sometimes wonder if they are worthy to partake of the sacrament despite having imperfections in their lives. The following provides some guidance for us concerning this question:

- **Continuously Repenting** – Elder John H. Groberg of the Seventy, speaking in the April 1989 general conference, said, **"If we are continuously repenting and improving, then we are worthy to partake of the sacrament."** Adding to this thought, Elder Lynn G. Robbins of the Seventy, in April 2018 said, "The sacrament is the Lord's designated way of providing continual access to His forgiveness. If we partake with a broken heart and a contrite spirit, **He offers us weekly pardon as we progress from failure to failure along the covenant path."**

- **Sacrament Restrictions** – Today's Church policies concerning worthiness, per the *General Handbook*, are that any priesthood holder who has committed a serious transgression should not be involved in the sacrament ordinance **until he has repented and resolved the problem with the bishop.** A similar type of restriction may apply to other Church members. If any member has committed a serious transgression, **the bishop may ask them to forego partaking of the sacrament for a period of time as part of the repentance process.**

- **Nonmembers and the Sacrament** – Some wonder about whether nonmembers should be offered the sacrament when they attend our meetings. The Church's current direction concerning this question is that, although the sacrament is for Church members, **bishoprics should not announce that it will only be passed to members, and they should not do anything to prevent others from partaking of it.**

- **Revision of Temple Recommend Questions** – In the October 2019 general conference, President Russell M. Nelson announced that some temple recommend questions had been revised and edited for clarity. Concerning sacrament worthiness, one of the questions now says, "Do you strive to keep the Sabbath day holy, both at home and at church; attend your meetings; **prepare for and worthily partake of the sacrament;** and live your life in harmony with the laws and commandments of the gospel?" (Previously, the question was, "Do you strive to keep the covenants you have made, to attend your sacrament and other meetings, and to keep your life in harmony with the laws and commandments of the gospel?")

In conclusion, worthiness has always been an important consideration if we are to participate in the sacred sacrament ordinance – either as one who is using the priesthood to prepare, bless, and pass it, or as one who has the privilege of partaking of the bread and water. As we attend our sacrament meetings and participate in the holy sacrament ordinance, we might do well to keep in mind Moroni's counsel in Mormon 9:29, which was quoted earlier: "See that ye are not baptized unworthily; **see that ye partake not of the sacrament of Christ unworthily;** but see that ye do all things in worthiness…"

(Note – Now, just a few additional thoughts about temple worthiness and temple recommends. **As stated before, temple recommends are not required in order for a person to partake of the sacrament.** Although they are not used for this aspect of Church participation, they are an important document used to signify our faithfulness and worthiness.

Temple recommends have an interesting history. In the early days of the Church, **each recommend was issued by the President of the Church.** This policy continued until the late 1800s when the signatures of a person's bishop and stake president on the recommend form provided authorization to go to the temple.

For many years, a recommend allowed just a single visit to a specific temple, not to all temples. The scope of a recommend was broadened over time, providing the holder entry into all temples as often as they wished to attend. And usage periods and expiration dates were introduced – for six months at first, then one year, and now two years.

Temple recommend worthiness questions have always been focused on a person's faithfulness, honesty, moral cleanliness, and Church service. But over the years, the individual questions have been adjusted, added to, or eliminated to match the times and circumstances. For instance, an interesting question used in the past to assess worthiness and gospel faithfulness during more agrarian times was, **"Have you cut hay where you had no right to, or turned animals into another person's grain field without his knowledge or consent?"** Another one was, **"Have you branded an animal that you did not know to be your own?"**)

Sacrament Term

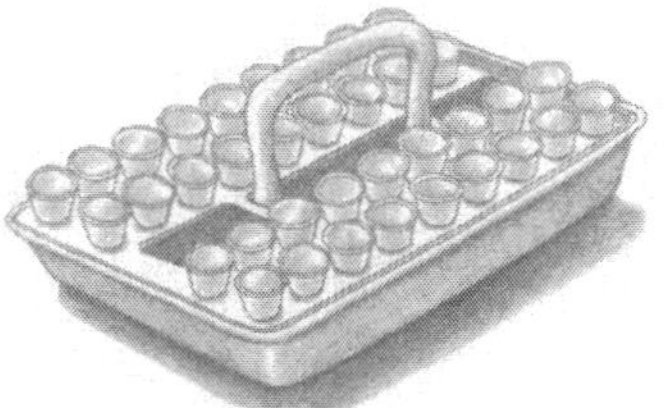

The Right Hand

A common sacrament-related question in The Church of Jesus Christ of Latter-day Saints is, "Is it necessary to take the sacrament with one's right hand?" As taught in the Church's *General Handbook,* **the answer is that members should partake with their right hand when possible.**

The right hand has been referred to in the Church as **the covenant hand,** therefore, as we perform ordinances and enter into covenants, the right hand (when possible) is used. In 1983, President Russell M. Nelson (who was a regional representative at that time), said the following in a talk:

> "Partaking of the sacrament might be thought of as a renewal by oath of the covenant previously made in the waters of baptism…The hand used in partaking of the sacrament would logically be the same hand used in making any other sacred oath. **For most of us, that would be the right hand.** However, sacramental covenants – and other eternal covenants as well – can be and are made by those who have lost the use of the right hand, or who have no hands at all."

He also talked about how parents are sometimes concerned with which hand their children use to partake of the sacrament. **He counseled that it is important to help children develop an understanding and a good feeling about the symbolism and significance of the sacrament,** and said:

"Parents who wish to teach the importance of this sacred experience might make the topic (of which hand to use) a part of a family home evening instruction. Then, if a reminder becomes necessary in a meeting, it may be given quietly, in patience and love."

Renewing Our Covenants

As we partake of the sacrament, we renew our baptismal covenants. **What does that mean and what promises are contained in our baptismal covenants?**

If you are a member of The Church of Jesus Christ of Latter-day Saints, do you remember the interview you had before you were baptized and confirmed? Whether you were about to turn eight years of age and be baptized, or whether you were a convert who had been taught by the missionaries, **the baptismal interview was an essential step in the process of preparing yourself to enter into Christ's Church.** In that interview, questions were asked which helped determine if you were qualified and ready to accept the obligations of membership and to make important covenants with God.

Here are several of the questions that are asked in a baptismal interview:

- "Do you believe that God is our Eternal Father? Do you believe that Jesus Christ is the Son of God and the Savior and Redeemer of the world?

- Do you believe that the Church and gospel of Jesus Christ have been restored through the Prophet Joseph Smith? Do you believe that [current Church president] is a prophet of God? What does this mean to you?

- What does it mean to you to repent? Do you feel that you have repented of your past sins?
- You have been taught that membership in The Church of Jesus Christ of Latter-day Saints includes living gospel standards. What do you understand about the following standards? Are you willing to obey them?
  - The law of chastity, which prohibits any sexual relations outside the bonds of a legal marriage between a man and a woman
  - The law of tithing
  - The Word of Wisdom
  - Keeping the Sabbath day holy, including partaking of the sacrament weekly and serving others.
- **When you are baptized, you covenant with God that you are willing to take upon yourself the name of Christ, serve others, stand as a witness of God at all times, and keep His commandments throughout your life. Are you ready to make this covenant and strive to be faithful to it?"**

In the baptismal covenant, solemnly made in the name of the Father, the Son, and the Holy Ghost, **God promises the person**

being baptized a remission of their sins and redemption through the Atonement of Jesus Christ. The new member covenants with God to keep the commandments and to take upon themself the name of Christ (Mosiah 18:8-10; Doctrine and Covenants 20:37).

And then God provides us an unusual and special blessing after the baptism – the blessing that each week, at each sacrament meeting, we can renew this important covenant and refresh our promises to God as we worthily partake of the sacrament. **And as we do so, God tells us each time that we will always have His Spirit to be with us!**

Members of The Church of Jesus Christ of Latter-day Saints are a covenant-making people. In addition to baptismal covenants, we have covenants associated with the Melchizedek Priesthood, the temple endowment, and eternal marriage in the temple. In an October 2011 general conference address, **President Russell M. Nelson, then a member of the Quorum of the Twelve Apostles, emphasized the importance of covenants:**

> "One of the most important concepts of revealed religion is that of a sacred covenant…Through the ages, God has made covenants with His children. **His covenants occur throughout the entire plan of salvation and are therefore part of the fulness of His gospel…**When we realize that we are children of the covenant, we know who we are and what God expects of us. His law is written in our hearts. He is our God and we are His people. Committed children of the covenant remain steadfast, even in the midst of adversity. When that doctrine is deeply implanted in our hearts, even the sting of death is soothed and our spiritual stamina is strengthened. **The greatest compliment that can be earned here in this life is to be known as a covenant keeper.** The rewards of a covenant keeper will be realized both here and hereafter."

I am grateful for the sacrament, for baptismal covenants, and for all gospel covenants, and hope that I will always be found

118

to be a **covenant keeper** who has the importance of covenants deeply implanted in my heart.

(Note – An additional thought about renewing covenants is the idea that has been presented in some talks and articles over the years **that partaking of the sacrament renews all covenants, not just baptismal covenants.** Here are some examples of what has been said on that subject:

- **Elder Delbert L. Stapley,** October 1965 general conference: "By partaking of the sacrament **we renew all covenants** entered into with the Lord."
- **President Spencer W. Kimball,** *Teachings,* page 112: "Remembering covenants prevents apostasy. That is the real purpose of the sacrament, to keep us from forgetting, **to help us to remember that which we have covenanted at the water's edge or at the sacrament table and in the temple."**
- *I Have a Question*, March 1995 *Ensign:* "According to our latter-day prophets and leaders, when you partake of the sacrament you renew whatever covenants you have made with the Lord. For example, if you have been baptized only, that is the covenant you renew. If you have received the Melchizedek Priesthood, you also renew that part of the oath and covenant related to your having received that priesthood. If you have received your endowment, you also renew the covenants associated with it. Further, if you have been sealed, you also renew that covenant. **In other words, when you partake of the sacrament, you renew all the covenants you have made with the Lord."** (Note – Beginning in September 1973 and continuing for a number of years thereafter, *I Have a Question* was a monthly feature of the *Ensign* magazine. Readers were invited to submit questions which were then answered by gospel scholars and church leaders. The answers were "for general guidance and not as official statements of Church policy." The

March 1995 answer quoted here was provided by John E. McKay, a gospel doctrine teacher in a Salt Lake City ward.)

- **Sister Carole M. Stephens,** October 2013 general conference: "We need the opportunity to renew our covenants each week as we partake of the sacrament. Latter-day prophets and apostles have taught that **when we worthily partake of the sacrament, we can renew not only our baptismal covenant but 'all covenants entered into with the Lord.'"**

So, whether the sacrament helps us renew all covenants, or only baptismal covenants, the opportunity to partake of the sacrament weekly is one of the greatest blessings the gospel affords.)

Sacrament Term

To the Souls

Both sacrament prayers in The Church of Jesus Christ of Latter-day Saints include the phrase, "…to bless and sanctify this (bread/water) **to the souls of all those who (partake/drink) of it…**" The dictionary defines a soul as the spiritual or immaterial part of a human being. To Latter-day Saints, however, the word soul has a broader and more complete definition. Doctrine and Covenants 88:15 teaches that **"the spirit and the body are the soul of man."**

So, when Latter-day Saints partake of the sacrament, it is a blessing and a sanctification to their entire being (to their soul) – **to both their spirit and their body.**

Patent No. 1,156,319

A New and Useful Communion Service

On May 8, 1912, **Brother Jacob Schaub of Logan, Utah** (who converted to The Church of Jesus Christ of Latter-day Saints in Switzerland), filed a United States patent application for **"a new and useful communion service."** In the 5-page patent application, he described his product as follows:

> "This invention appertains to a communion service, and, more particularly, to means whereby individual containers may be thoroughly sterilized after the containers shall have been used and without risk of breakage or injury to said containers."

In plainer words, his invention was a device that would wash and sterilize individual metal sacrament cups after they had been used in sacrament meetings. Designed to handle 144 cups at a time, it also provided a method for the user to place the small sterilized cups back into the sacrament trays **without human hands ever touching them.** Here are the drawings that accompanied the patent application for his device:

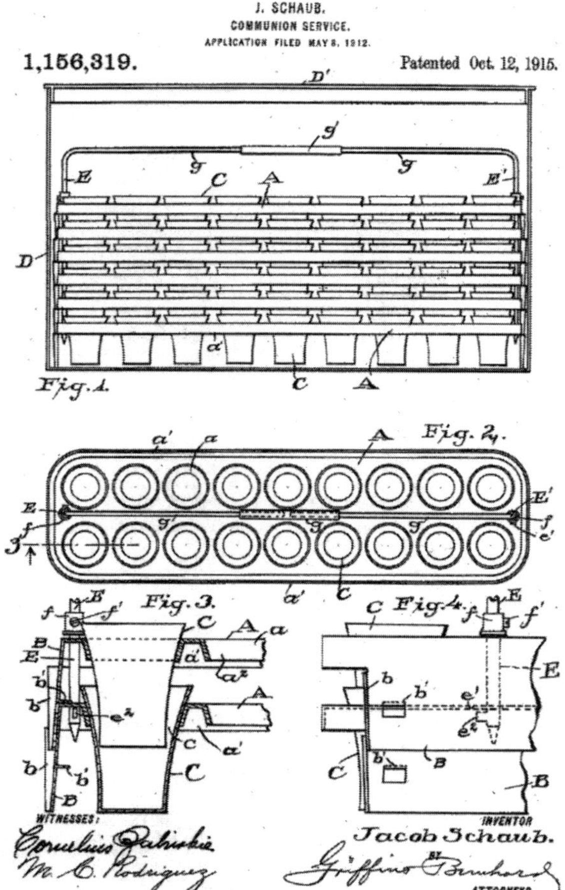

Brother Schaub's application for the communion service was approved by the government and was assigned U. S. Patent No. 1,156,319. In addition to his sterilizing device, Schaub also made metal water trays and small individual metal sacrament cups in his machine shop in Logan. And, he placed something rather unusual and distinctive on the bottom of his little cups. In tiny lettering on each one he stamped the words, **"Made for Deseret Sunday School Union – By Jacob Schaub, Logan, Utah."**

Sacrament-related Products

With the movement by the Church towards using individual sacrament cups, **the wards and branches needed to obtain small sacrament cups and trays that would accommodate those cups.** It wasn't long, therefore, before a number of products came into the Latter-day Saint market to satisfy these and other sacrament-related needs. Many of these items proved to be of great benefit to the units of the Church in their efforts to make the new way of partaking of the sacrament as sanitary, efficient, and reverent as possible. Over time, these new products included:

- Small cups made of a variety of materials.
- Water trays of many designs, configurations, and materials.
- Bread trays to match the new water trays.
- Products to help improve both how to prepare and how to take down the sacrament.
- Traveling sacrament kits.

Let's take a look at two interesting examples of these types of products.

(1) Water Filling Device

Among the various water filling devices that were developed, one metal one with an attached hose was particularly clever. **It consisted of four stainless-steel tubes welded together, a metal valve, and a short length of rubber hose.** Its purpose was to enable those filling the cups prior to the meeting to precisely control the amount of water that went into each cup in order to eliminate overfilling and spilling.

The filler was designed to be attached to a water faucet in a meetinghouse's kitchen or sacrament preparation room. To fill the sacrament cups, one end of the flexible hose was attached to the device, the other end was screwed onto the faucet, and the water was turned on. After the four metal tubes were carefully positioned directly over the 36 empty cups in a water tray, **the person filling the cups would push the metal control valve, which allowed the proper amount of water to flow into each sacrament cup through the 36 small holes drilled in the bottom of the device's stainless-steel tubes.**

(2) Miniature Traveling Sacrament Kit

Another useful idea was that of traveling sacrament kits. **They were developed so members, when authorized to do so, could reverently partake of the sacrament away from a meetinghouse much the same way they did when at a regular sacrament meeting.** The kits, which came in various designs and sizes, enabled bishops to more easily assign priesthood holders to take the sacrament to home-bound members, hospitalized members, those in nursing homes and care centers, or others living away from meetinghouses. Such kits were also utilized by those serving in the military.

One particularly extra-small kit was rather ingenious. Packaged in a zippered case that measured just 5 inches by 5 inches by 2½ inches, **this miniature sacrament service contained everything needed to provide the sacrament away from a meetinghouse** – a bread tray, a water tray, several sacrament cups in a plastic container, a plastic container for bread, a two-sided prayer card, and two small white cotton cloths – all nested together in a water-repellent protective case. It was invented by a member of the Church in California.

Summary

Over the years, many sacrament-related products have been developed for the wards and branches of the Church.

While many of these were done under the direction and sponsorship of the Church itself, others came from interested companies and individuals working on their own. These new products – cups, trays, and other devices – were helpful to the Church as this new era of the sacrament came into being. **This also was a period of time when the leaders of the Church focused even more than before on refining, improving, and standardizing the procedures, policies, practices, and methods of holding sacrament meetings and of administering the sacrament.**

And, because we live in a rapidly evolving world and because The Church of Jesus Christ of Latter-day Saints is led by ongoing revelation and inspiration, **perhaps additional refinements and changes in the way the sacrament ordinance is conducted might take place in the future** – all with the purpose of helping us improve our worship and better remember and appreciate the Savior and His Atonement.

Additional Notes

Brother Schaub's metal cups, sacrament trays, and communion sterilization service were quite popular in the Church for a number of years, but as individual cups made of glass and other materials and improved water tray designs were developed by others, his inventions became less and less needed and he stopped making them. **However, he never lost his desire to invent things, and by the end of his life Schaub had obtained a total of 33 patents,** some while he was self-employed and some while working for others. Interestingly, while affiliated with a company in another state, he was instrumental in developing a product used by soldiers in World War I. It enabled them to heat their food rations while out on the battlefield. The product went through several improvements and name changes and was eventually marketed commercially as **Sterno.** No doubt you've heard of it and perhaps have used it yourself.

There have also been a number of **non-Latter-day Saint** sacrament or communion-related inventions over the years. Two that I found of particular interest were:

(1) Gel Capsule

In 2003, a patent application was submitted for a **communion gel capsule** that could be swallowed like one takes medication. The capsule had two separate interior cavities – one containing sacrament wine and the other containing a sacrament wafer. The patent application said, "This would allow the elements of communion to be compact, portable, conveniently transportable, and distributable so that a user can participate in the communion ritual both away from and during church."

(2) Edible Cup

An application in 2016 was filed for an **edible communion cup.** The cup was made from carbohydrates coated with an edible wax. It contained the sacrament liquid and was enclosed and sealed tightly on top with a communion wafer. The wording accompanying the application said, "In use, the common wafer is removed and consumed with the liquid to satisfy the requirements of the sacrament. The cup may also then be consumed to avoid any waste."

Sacrament Term

Bakelite

Several of the old sacrament cups I have in my collection are made of Bakelite. They are light tan in color and have the appearance of plastic. Along with glass, metal, paper, and other types of plastic, Bakelite is one of the substances that has been used over the years to make individual sacrament cups.

Bakelite is noteworthy because it was the first plastic made totally from synthetic components. Developed in New York in 1907 by Leo Baekeland, a Belgian-American chemist, it has a number of important properties – it can be molded quickly, its surface is very smooth, it retains its shape for a long time, and it is resistant to scratches and heat. **As such, it proved to be an excellent material for small sacrament cups.** Many products in the 1900s were made of Bakelite, including radio cases, kitchenware, jewelry, toys, and electrical insulators. The old black rotary dial telephone in our kitchen as I grew up was made of Bakelite.

And for those of you who like details, the chemical name for Bakelite is **polyoxybenzylmethylenglycolanhydride.**

The Most Important Building in Our Town

Elder David B. Haight, who was born in 1906 and passed away in 2004 at the age of 97, grew up in the small town of Oakley, Idaho. At the time of his passing, he had been a member of the Quorum of the Twelve Apostles for 28 years. In a 1983 general conference talk about the sacrament, he said the following:

"I wish everyone could grow up in a small town. I have so many happy memories from my boyhood…**The most important building in our town in addition to the schoolhouse was our ward meetinghouse.** The chapel had an imposing, two-tiered, elevated stand. The stand was quite large, and the first raised portion had a table for the ward clerk at one end and a piano at the other end, **and right in the center of this elevated area was the sacrament table.** On the highest level of the stand was the pulpit with its red plush cover and beautifully carved chairs with red plush seats for the bishopric or visiting authorities… **Everyone in attendance had a clear view of the stately pulpit and, of course, the sacrament table.** After the sacrament song had been sung, the priests knelt on a little red velvet bench as they offered the blessing on the bread and water. We didn't have printed cards, but the twentieth section of the Doctrine and Covenants was open if needed. There were no microphones or speakers."

The meetinghouse that Elder Haight attended as a young boy in Oakley, Idaho was built in 1902 out of native stone from the surrounding area. Used until 1953, it stood as a beautiful and important landmark until it was destroyed by fire in 1965. The organ from the meetinghouse was preserved and is on display in the town's museum. Here is a photograph of that wonderful old building that meant so much to Elder Haight.

The meetinghouses of The Church of Jesus Christ of Latter-day Saints have always been a great blessing to the members of the Church. Providing an important spiritual and temporal environment in which to worship and participate in the various aspects of the gospel, the designs of the buildings are a reflection of our doctrines, beliefs, and practices. Over the years, our buildings, and particularly the ways we use them, have changed as the Church and its programs have expanded and matured. A review of the history of several architectural elements of our meetinghouses that pertain to the sacrament ordinance gives us a glimpse into this.

- **Sacrament Tables** – Initially, our worship services were held in homes, schools, borrowed facilities, and the like. **The tables used for the sacrament in those places were simple everyday tables that were normally already present in those facilities, rather than tables that were specially designed and built for the sacrament ordinance.** When the first Latter-day Saint meetinghouses were constructed in the 1800s, portable tables, as opposed to built-in sacrament tables, were typical. When not being used in the chapel for sacrament meeting, they were often moved to another area of the building and used for other purposes. As the design of Latter-day Saint meetinghouses progressed, **built-in, non-movable sacrament tables became part of the configuration of our chapels.** Standard meetinghouse plans had not yet been developed by the Church, so architects were free to make the tables whatever size seemed proper and to place them wherever they seemed to fit best – typically on elevated platforms in the middle of the chapel directly under the pulpit, as in Elder Haight's building in Oakley.

  Today, standardized building plans have been developed for our meetinghouses, **so the arrangement of the stands in the chapel and the placement and size of sacrament tables is largely similar throughout our buildings.** For example, in our ward's chapel, the placement of the pulpit, choir seats, and sacrament table seems to be quite typical. The pulpit is at the front and center of the chapel on a raised platform. A piano, organ, and several rows of choir seats are also on the stand – as is a built-in table for a clerk. Our sacrament table is at the front of the chapel on the right side when facing the pulpit and is on a riser that is one step above the congregation. (The exact placement of the table can vary from plan to plan. Some are on the left, some are on the right, some are on the same level as the congregation, and some are raised a step or two. Seldom in newer buildings, however, are sacrament tables located in the middle of the chapel below the pulpit as they once were.) The dimensions of our building's sacrament table are 72" long x 32" inches deep x 40" high (which is quite standard), and an upholstered bench wide enough to seat four priests is positioned directly behind the sacrament table (which also is quite standard).

Facilities and conveniences to help in preparing the sacrament were not included in early meetinghouse designs. For instance, providing water for the sacrament was sometimes a bit of a task before running water was available in our buildings. An article in the May 1911 *Improvement Era* talked about this:

> "(Sacrament) water should be the purest obtainable, and in those country districts, where of necessity the supply must be obtained from streams, care should be taken that no foreign substances are present to offend the sensitive."

I've read several historical accounts about how some building custodians in the early days of the Church had the assignment to draw water from nearby streams early enough on Sunday mornings so any impurities in the water had sufficient time to either settle to the bottom of the pail or float to the surface before the start of the meeting. The custodian would then carefully scoop the floating contaminants from the top of the water before ladling the remaining clear water near the surface into large sacrament pitchers that were placed on the sacrament table.

- **Sacrament Preparation Rooms** – Special facilities to aid in the preparation of the sacrament were typically not included in our meetinghouses until several decades into the 1900s. **These proved to be very popular, so from about**

1950 on, virtually all new Latter-day Saint meetinghouses had a formal sacrament preparation room. Usually located at the back of the stand on either side of the organ pipes, these rooms typically consisted of a sink, cold water faucet, countertop, and several cupboards for the storage of trays, cups, and sacrament linens. Eventually, some sacrament preparation rooms were located in hallways adjacent to the chapel rather than on the stand. This allowed for those preparing the sacrament to do so without disturbing any meetings or classes that were taking place in the chapel.

The sacrament preparation room in the meetinghouse where my wife and I attend church is one of these. Situated in the hallway next to the chapel, our little preparation room includes a handy additional feature found only in some Latter-day Saint buildings – a pass-through window. Built into the wall between the sacrament preparation room and the chapel **is a small opening with a hinged door that can be opened and closed.** Measuring 22" wide x 26 " high, the portal allows for sacrament trays to be prepared and filled in the sacrament preparation room and then handed through the small window to someone standing by the sacrament table so the trays can be placed on the sacrament table without having to carry them out into the hall and into the chapel.

- **Microphones** – The introduction of microphones on the pulpits in chapels was a great blessing to the Church, **and now most meetinghouses also have a microphone located at the sacrament table** so the sacrament prayers can be easily heard by the congregation. Some of these microphones are on a cord and are simply placed on the table. Others are built-in. One such built-in device seen in some meetinghouses is part of a clever microphone system located at the upper back edge of the sacrament table. With this feature, when it is time to say the sacrament prayer, the priest pulls down a small hinged metal plate. Doing so activates a microphone and also uncovers a card on which the sacrament prayers are printed. The priest kneels down and says the prayer into the microphone. When finished, he pushes the hinged plate back up, which turns off the microphone. The trays can then be handed to the deacons without having any noise associated with that function picked up by the microphone.

- **Non-standard Designs** – Some of our meetinghouses over the years have had some interesting non-standard design elements in them. For instance:

  - **Two Sacrament Tables** – The Arlington, Virginia meetinghouse located at 1600 N. Inglewood Street has two sacrament tables. At the time of its dedication in 1947, it was the only Latter-day Saint building in the greater Washington, D.C. area. Because it was anticipated that the building would need to accommodate a larger-than-normal congregation, the architect (Orel Rasband) received permission to include two sacrament tables in the design. **Sitting in the congregation facing the pulpit, the table on the right side of the chapel is used for the bread and the table on the left for the water.** Four priests are assigned to the sacrament, two at each table. After the bread is blessed, the deacons get up from their seats located on the front pew in the center of the chapel and stand at the table on the right to obtain their trays. After passing the bread, they return those trays to that same table and stand at that table while the two priests at the water table on the other side of the chapel bless the water. The deacons then move to the water table to obtain those trays. They return them to that table after the water has been passed. The deacons then return to their pew at the front of the chapel until the one conducting the meeting dismisses them. Today, the ward still uses both sacrament tables in their services. (Note – The foregoing information was provided by Linda Wardle, a long-time member of the ward, and Barry Merrell, a former member of the ward.)

- o **A Sacrament Table with Two Tiers** – As I grew up, my ward had an unusually large number of members, so our meetinghouse was built with a larger-than-normal sacrament table – **a two-tiered one.** Rather than facing towards the congregation like most sacrament tables, it was built parallel to the left wall of the chapel and faced sideways. The table had a large wooden top on which the bread trays were placed – plus it had a long glass shelf above the wooden table on which the water trays were set. This beautiful two-tiered table effectively served the sacrament needs of our large congregation – although as a deacon, I did notice two things about its use that were a bit unusual. First, short priests had some difficulty reaching the water trays that were on the far side of the glass shelf, and second, the sacrament table cloth was an unusually large one so it could properly cover both tiers of sacrament trays. Folding it up after the service was not an easy thing for the young Aaronic Priesthood boys to do. (Note – My building was not unique in this regard. A number of other older meetinghouses have also had two-tiered sacrament tables.)

- o **One Sacrament Table Between Two Pulpits** – The Kalaupapa, Hawaii meetinghouse, located on the island of Molokai, was built with one sacrament table and two pulpits – **one pulpit for "patients" and one for "visitors."** In 1866, Hawaii designated Molokai as the site for a leper colony. (You might remember hearing about Father Damien who served as a Catholic priest there for 16 years.) A number of "patients" in the colony were members of The

Church of Jesus Christ of Latter-day Saints and over the years a succession of small chapels were built by the Church on the island to provide services for them. One of these chapels, called the Kalaupapa meetinghouse, was designed so that "patients" with leprosy sat on the left side of the chapel and used the pulpit on their side, while any "visitors" to the branch sat on the other side and used the pulpit on their side. The sacrament table was situated in the middle between the two pulpits. Although quite a small meetinghouse which would normally require only one restroom, the building had two – one designated for "patients" and one set aside for "visitors." (Note – The information about Kalaupapa was provided by Julian and Momilani Kau and the Ka 'Ohana O Kalaupapa Society.)

Latter-day Saint meetinghouses are a wonderful and special benefit to the members of the Church. The meetinghouse that Holly and I attend each Sunday is a beautiful building located a short distance from our home. Although it is just one of several Latter-day Saint meetinghouses in our community, we consider this particular one to be very special – because it is "ours." A warm and inviting building, we enjoy going there to worship, partake of the sacrament, receive instruction, and associate with our brothers and sisters in the gospel. **Similar to how Elder Haight felt about his building in Oakley, Idaho, we are grateful for our meetinghouse and consider it to be one of the most important buildings in our town.**

(Note – My family has a bit of a historical connection to the town of Oakley, Idaho where Elder Haight was born. My great-grandparents on my mother's side lived there and are buried in the Oakley cemetery. My grandparents lived there for a short time, as did my mother and several of my aunts and uncles. And, my sister and brother-in-law and their children, who, interestingly, have the last name of **Ockey**, lived in **Oakley** for five years while my brother-in-law taught seminary there.)

Sacrament Term

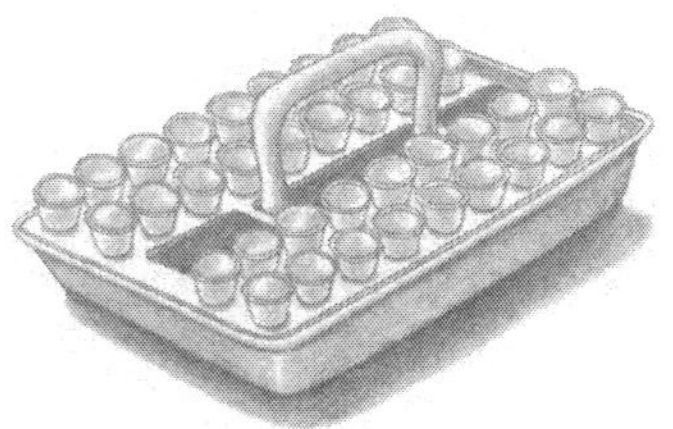

Sacraments

The Church of Jesus Christ of Latter-day Saints has the sacrament (singular). Many other Christian churches have **sacraments (plural).** For them, a sacrament is a visible religious rite, ritual, ceremony, or observance – not just the celebration of the Lord's Supper.

For instance, the number of sacraments in the Catholic Church has varied over time, but since the mid-13th century, they have recognized **seven sacraments** – baptism, confirmation, the Eucharist, penance, anointing the sick, holy orders, and matrimony. Most Protestant churches recognize **two sacraments** – baptism and communion. However, the Community of Christ (formerly the Reorganized Church of Jesus Christ of Latter Day Saints) practices **eight sacraments** – baptism, confirmation, the Lord's Supper, ordination, blessing of children, laying on of hands for the sick, marriage, and the evangelist's blessing.

Revive Inactive Members

I got a bit of a chuckle when I read a 1933 list of priesthood duties for teachers in the Aaronic Priesthood. One of the twenty responsibilities listed was to **revive inactive members.** That's certainly an interesting way to talk about bringing members back into Church participation. (Later in the chapter we'll take a look at the list.)

In today's Church, the details of Aaronic Priesthood responsibilities, including how to properly administer the sacrament, are contained in the Church's *General Handbook.* Over the years, the *General Handbook* has grown from just a few pages, all in English, to a sizable document available in over 51 languages. First published in 1899 and called ***Instructions to Presidents of Stakes, Bishops of Wards and Stake Tithing Clerks,*** it contained just 14 pages and talked primarily about how to handle tithing in kind – **such as answering the interesting question about what bishops should do with a live pig that has been offered as tithing.**

As it has grown in size and scope, the book has gone by various names, such as *Annual Instructions,* then *General Handbook of Instructions,* and now *General Handbook.* (The actual full name of the present document is, ***General Handbook: Serving in The Church of Jesus Christ of Latter-day Saints.***) In 2020, this valuable resource "adapted to the ministerial needs of a global faith" (per a news release by the Church), **became digital** only and was made available online to all Church members as well as to the general public.

The *General Handbook* covers many important topics, including, of course, the sacrament. An important principle taught in the handbook about the sacrament is that the keys for administering the sacrament in the ward or branch are held by the bishop or branch president and that all who participate in preparing, blessing, and passing the sacrament must receive approval from the bishop or branch president, or someone under their direction.

Concerning the preparation function of the sacrament ordinance, today's guidelines indicate that this is a priesthood responsibility. Teachers, priests, and those who hold the Melchizedek Priesthood may prepare the sacrament. Their duty is to make sure that before the meeting starts, clean and pressed white table cloths are on the sacrament table, clean bread trays with unbroken bread are in place, and clean water trays with cups of clean water are set on the table. **After the meeting, the *General Handbook* specifies that those who prepared the sacrament are to take down the sacrament.**

The fact that the preparation of the sacrament is a priesthood responsibility is well understood in today's Church, but it has not always been so. The specific guidelines and details relating to the sacrament ordinance, including the preparation of the sacrament, have evolved during the more than 190 years the Church has been restored. Doctrine and Covenants Section 20, revealed in 1830 at the time the Church was organized, **gave doctrinal information about the duties of priesthood holders** (verses 38 through 67) and it also gave us the words to be used in the sacrament prayers (verses 77 and 79) – **but there are only a few instructions in the scriptures relating to how to carry out those duties.**

Rather, over time, the specific instructions for the sacrament have been given to the Church line upon line and precept upon precept, often coming to us, not in the *General Handbook*, but by way of talks from leaders, articles in Church magazines and periodicals, and priesthood bulletins. Today, of course, the

General Handbook is the instrument the Church uses to cover all of these things.

For instance, if we need information concerning who should receive the sacrament first, which hand should be used to partake of the sacrament, or the role music plays relating to the sacrament ordinance, **we turn to the *General Handbook* for the answers.** Concerning those three questions, today's handbook provides the following instructions: The presiding leader receives the sacrament first, **after which there is no set order.** Members should partake **with their right hand when possible.** As the bread is being broken, a sacrament hymn is to be sung **by the congregation,** not by the choir or by a soloist.

To help illustrate the line upon line and precept upon precept progression of sacrament policies over the years, let's look at several items of historical information relating to the specific subject of **sacrament preparation**:

- **Sacrament Preparation in the Early Years of the Church**
  There is not a great deal of information about who was involved in the preparation of the sacrament during the early years of the Church, but it does appear from what is found in journals, meeting minutes, and other accounts, that many people were involved in this responsibility. Even women played a role at times as they helped furnish and prepare the sacrament emblems and placed linens and trays on the table. In Hartley's previously mentioned article, *From Men to Boys,* he tells about a woman named Kate Coreless, a member of the 4th Ward in Salt Lake City, who "took care of the sacrament table for a quarter of a century after 1906. She crocheted the cloth, polished the silver trays, baked and sliced the bread, and set the sacrament table."

- **Practical Duties for Members of the Lesser Priesthood in 1916**

A July 1916 article in the *Improvement Era* talked about the practical duties for members of the Lesser Priesthood. In a section called, **"Priesthood Quorums' Table,"** it read:

> "Recently the bishops of the Church were asked, through letters sent out by the Presiding Bishopric, what activities were engaged in by members of the Lesser Priesthood in the different wards. The answers, with a number added by the committee, were compiled from which the Priesthood committee makes the following suggestions, hoping they will be of service to bishops throughout the Church, many of whom have found difficulty in providing activities for members of the Aaronic Priesthood quorums."

Among the activities listed for teachers in the Lesser Priesthood, we find the suggestion that they should:

- Assist in ward teaching
- **Assist with the sacrament**
- See that the service is in order
- Become instructors for boy scouts
- Collect ward funds
- Serve as choir members
- Serve as ushers in gatherings
- Be order monitors

It is interesting to note that, although the list mentions that teachers should **assist with the sacrament,** it does not specifically say in what manner they should do so – and it does not use the words **"prepare the sacrament."**

- **1930s Young Girls MIA Assignment**

In Brother Hartley's article mentioned previously, he relates the story of Annette Steeneck Huntington who was a member of the Salt Lake Emigration Stake during the 1930s. Sister Huntington said "that during the 1930s in the

Emigration Stake, the young girls in MIA filled the water cups in the kitchen and placed the bread on the trays. We then prepared the Sacrament table with the cloth and trays on it. **It was a wonderful privilege I shall always remember."**

- **1933 List of Priesthood Duties**
As mentioned at the start of the chapter, in 1933 a list of priesthood duties came out. Appearing in the December issue of the *Improvement Era* under the heading **"Assignments for Ordained Teachers" it included the duty of preparing the sacrament table.** Prior to this time, there appears to have been **no official mention** of preparing the table being a specific priesthood duty. The article said there had been some misunderstandings regarding the assignments for teachers in the Aaronic Priesthood. It then spelled out a list of twenty duties for teachers. Here are ten of the twenty duties:

  - Ward teaching
  - Attend sacrament meeting
  - **Prepare sacrament table**
  - Assist at cottage meetings
  - Messenger for bishop
  - Usher
  - Collect ward funds
  - Prepare meeting house
  - Cut wood
  - And the intriguing assignment to **<u>revive</u> inactive members**

- **Girls "Pinch-Hit" for Deacons**
An April 21, 1945 article in the *Church News* titled *Girls "Pinch-Hit" for Deacons* contained a photo of ten "Bee-Hive" girls wearing bandalos. Although not about sacrament preparation, the short article talked about another typical priesthood function, that of collecting fast offerings,

that was done by persons not holding the priesthood. The short article said:

> "Two years ago the man-power shortage reached down even into the deacon's quorum of the Aaronic Priesthood of the Twenty-Fourth (Salt Lake City) Ward and left them without enough boys to collect fast offerings. **Bishop Oscar M. Olson turned to a group of Bee-Hive Girls for assistance,** and under the leadership of their Bee-Keeper, Naoma Sorenson, they have collected fast offerings in a district comprising one half of the ward. During the past two years they did not once fail to cover their entire district. **Now with an increase in boys in the deacon's quorum the girls are, rather reluctantly, turning this job back to the priesthood.**"

- **The Role of Custodians**
Many meetinghouses during the early to middle 1900s had custodians. My growing-up ward had a custodian who worked diligently to keep the building clean, orderly, and in good repair. At times, I seem to recall that he came to the building quite early on Sunday mornings and beat the members of the teachers quorum to the task of preparing the sacrament before church started.

- **In the Netherlands in the Early 1950s**
I was born in Salt Lake City, but from 1952 to 1956 I lived in the Netherlands. Our family attended a branch in The Hague. **Although I was only of Primary age during those years,** along with my mother, sisters, and brother, I remember carrying the sacrament trays into the building's kitchen at the end of Sunday School and sacrament meeting and then helping wash and dry the individual glass sacrament cups so they would be ready for the next sacrament service. While I didn't like doing dishes at

home, I loved washing the sacrament cups at the meetinghouse.

- **Teachers to Prepare the Sacrament Table**
  The April 2, 1950 edition of the *Church News*, carried the following article from the Presiding Bishopric relating to the preparation of the sacrament:

  "It is recommended that ordained Teachers be given the responsibility of preparing the

sacrament table. This would include filling the cups in the water trays and the placing of unbroken bread in the bread trays, placing these on the sacrament table after clean linens have been placed, seeing that the trays are also covered after they have been placed on the table.

It is preferred that this particular responsibility not be delegated either to LDS girls or their mothers. Custodians should not be required to perform this service. Bearers of the Aaronic Priesthood should be assigned to look after this detail of the administration of the sacrament in both Sunday School and sacrament meeting."

Thus, **from 1950 on,** the teachers in the Aaronic Priesthood have had the clear and specific assignment in the Church to prepare the sacrament table.

These are just a few stories and examples to help illustrate the point **that policies and guidelines concerning the preparation of the sacrament (as well as other sacrament-related duties) grew line upon line and precept upon precept over the years.** I am grateful for today's guidelines and instructions that apply to all Church units around the world. I like that wherever we attend church, the sacrament experience is essentially the same. I appreciate the quiet and reverent time set aside each week for the partaking of the sacrament, and am grateful to the holders of the priesthood who so diligently prepare, bless, and pass the sacrament to us.

And I'm all for having the teachers in the Aaronic Priesthood continue with the assignment to <u>revive</u> inactive members.

Sacrament Term

Communion Casserole

Latter-day Saints aren't the only ones with a famous casserole. Our funeral potatoes are quite renowned, **and so is the Amish's communion casserole.**

Amish religious services take place weekly in a member's home. **Twice per year at those meetings – once in the spring and once in the fall – they take communion (the sacrament).** The regular service on those occasions is expanded into a special meeting which lasts several hours longer than normal. Due to the length of the service, which takes up most of the day, a lunch break is included. **In a number of Amish communities, it is traditional to serve a casserole called communion casserole as the main dish at the luncheon.**

The recipe for communion casserole can vary – much as the recipe for our funeral potatoes can – but the ingredients in a typical Amish communion casserole include cooked and diced chicken, bread cut into cubes, lightly beaten eggs, mayonnaise, milk, and chopped bell peppers, onions, and celery. Salt, pepper, and other seasonings are mixed in and then the ingredients are placed in a casserole dish. Shredded cheese is sprinkled on top, after which the casserole is cooked in large roasters.

The service consists of sermons, prayers, and scripture readings, with the actual communion taking place in the afternoon. **The bread and wine are distributed, after which the congregation sings a hymn about the washing of feet.** During the hymn, the deacon brings out buckets of warm water and towels **so that the members in attendance can wash each other's feet**

as a sign of humility and brotherhood. The foot washing concludes the communion service.

These twice-annual communion meetings are considered to be the highest and holiest moments of the Amish church calendar.

(Note – Hymns at Amish religious services come from the **Ausbund hymnal.** Used by the early Anabaptist Swiss Brethren, the hymnal was first printed in 1564 and is the oldest songbook in the world still in continuous use. **The hymn book does not contain any musical notes.** Instead, the tunes are learned by ear and are passed down from one generation to the next. At an Amish service, a song leader begins the hymn by singing the opening notes, after which the congregation joins in. The hymns are typically sung quite slowly with drawn-out notes.)

The Dripless Design

My father liked to tell people that both his first and last church assignment was to pass the sacrament. Born in 1906, Dad's first church responsibility as a brand-new deacon was to pass the sacrament in his Salt Lake City ward. After Mom passed away, Dad spent his later years in an assisted living center where he was again assigned to pass the sacrament. He loved doing so. **One time, Dad told me how grateful he was for the new water trays with their dripless design.** He said that in his youth, try as he might, little beads of excess water would sometimes run off the top of the tray and spill onto the lap of the person he was passing the sacrament to. Many decades later, as an adult in his 90s passing the sacrament in the center, he was appreciative of the water trays with the **dripless design** that largely prevented water from running off onto the sacrament recipient.

On a recent Sunday, in the midst of the COVID-19 pandemic, my wife and I partook of the sacrament in our home using **a small plastic sacrament tray that was made on a three-dimensional printer.** This tiny tray doubled as both the bread and water tray. **The two small plastic cups that came with the tray, were likewise made on a 3D printer. Who would have ever thought?** Our little sacrament meeting, which was a reverent and sacred experience, helped emphasize how sacrament trays and cups of today are very different from those used when the Savior instituted the sacrament and from those used when the sacrament ordinance was restored during the time of Joseph Smith.

During the Savior's day, and in the early years of this dispensation, **the vessels used in the sacrament ordinance were very simple and were not specifically made for the sacrament.** In the early decades of the restoration, items found in a typical kitchen or dining room were used – a metal or wood plate, a cup or goblet, and perhaps a basket of some sort. **Over time, as congregations grew, wards and branches began making their own trays and sacrament implements – or they purchased them from local merchants and mail order catalogs.** Several examples of early store-bought trays are:

- **Landers, Frary & Clark** – Landers, Frary & Clark, a housewares company in New Britain, Connecticut, made the trays that were used for many years as bread trays in one of Salt Lake City's oldest meetinghouses. **Those beautiful round metal trays with a sculpted design and collapsible metal handle, were marketed as candy dishes or finger food trays, not sacrament trays.** Landers, Frary & Clark operated from 1865 until its assets were sold to General Electric in 1965. They manufactured a wide variety of high-end consumer products including cutlery, cookware, candy dishes, and percolators. The company's name and the model number of the dish were stamped on the bottom of the sacrament trays used by the ward.

- **Indiana Glass Company** – A lead-cut crystal tray from the Indiana Glass Company was a beautiful feature of the weekly sacrament service in a meetinghouse located a few miles north of Salt Lake City. **The dish, used as a bread tray by the ward, was 9-inches by 9-inches in size with a bright steel handle that clamped onto two corners of the dish.** This striking tray had numerous crystal facets that provided a brilliant sparkle and shine. The Indiana Glass Company (located in Indiana, Pennsylvania) was a leading crystal glass company from the late 1800s until the early 1900s.

- **Knickerbocker Silver Company** – An old meetinghouse in southern Utah had heavy, round, well-used silverplate bread trays for the sacrament. Each tray had stamped on the bottom, **"Manufactured and Guaranteed by Knickerbocker Silver Co., High Grade Metal."** Also on the bottom was a stamped male figure wearing a colonial-style tricorn hat next to the stamp of an arm. The arm had a large biceps muscle and the hand at the end of the arm was holding a big hammer. The tray was silverplate, not sterling silver, because Knickerbocker, who did business from 1904 to 1962, did not make sterling silver items.

With the introduction in the Church of individual sacrament cups in 1911, a number of private companies began designing water trays specifically for The Church of Jesus Christ of Latter-day Saints. Soon, many of these companies introduced matching bread trays, resulting in most wards and branches during the early to middle 1900s having matching bread and water trays which were almost always made of metal. **In those years, Church units purchased sacrament trays on their own,** either directly from outside vendors or from Church-related entities such as Temple Square's Bureau of Information or Deseret Book.

Early water trays presented several challenges, two of which were: **(1) Where do we place the used water cups?** and **(2) How do we keep water from sliding off the tray and onto the lap of the one taking the sacrament?** A number of different styles of water trays made their way into wards and branches over the years, with each manufacturer hoping to overcome those two (and other) problems so they could become the preferred choice for Church units. Eventually, cup receptacles on top of the trays or space under or inside the trays were added to the designs to house the used cups so as to solve the first issue – and to solve the second challenge, elevated ridges or rims along the outer edges of the water trays were included to reduce water spillage. **The trays with the ridge or rim were often referred to as the dripless design.**

Eventually, as more and more Church units were formed around the world, the Church centralized the purchasing of sacrament trays, making it possible for wards and branches to obtain well-designed and approved standard sacrament trays without having to shop for them on their own. **Initially, all trays provided by the Church were made of metal.** Today, the approved bread and water trays that wards and branches order from the Church are made of **durable lightweight plastic.**

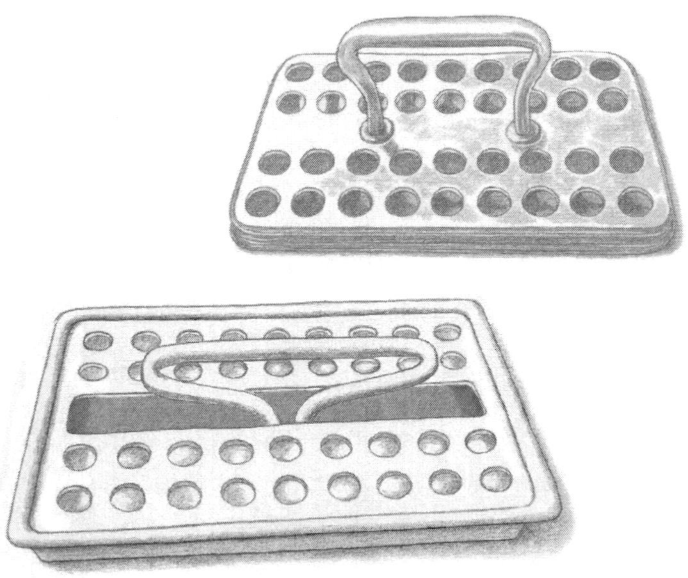

For many years, the small individual cups used for the sacrament were made of various substances **such as metal, glass, Bakelite, or other hard plastics.** These cups were eventually replaced by more sanitary **small pleated white paper cups** which were used one time and then discarded after each sacrament service. The paper cups were produced by private vendors and then shipped in bulk to Church Distribution in Salt Lake City. Individual Church entities from around the world would place orders with Church headquarters who would then ship the cups to where they were needed.

While in Hong Kong as a young missionary, I served for six months in the office of the Southern Far East Mission as the mission commissarian. I was responsible for the supplies for the mission, which included the sacrament cups for Church units throughout Southeast Asia. One week, it was discovered that many of the branches were low on sacrament cups (back then, we only had branches in the mission and no wards) because I had underestimated how many the mission used each week. We quickly had to order several big boxes of cups from Salt Lake and have them shipped by air freight to Hong Kong. Thankfully, the new supply arrived just before we totally ran out.

When small individual **single-use disposable soft plastic cups became feasible for the sacrament in the latter part of the 20th century, the Church largely moved from** paper cups to plastic cups. Because of the size of the Church and the growing number of members (more than 16 million members in over 31,000 congregations), **the Church invested in its own plastic sacrament cup production machine rather than purchase the cups it needed from outside vendors.** This interesting piece of equipment, located in Salt Lake City in the Church's main printing center, turns long rolls of food-grade plastic sheeting into small sacrament cups which are then shipped throughout the globe to fill the sacrament cup needs of the Church. (The machine has the capacity to make several million cups per day.)

There have been many changes in sacrament trays and cups since the ordinance was first instituted. The changes have been a blessing to the Church as it strives to make the sacrament more readily available to all and to increase the sacredness and special nature of the ordinance. Personally, I am grateful for the easy-to-use, well-designed, and hygienic sacrament vessels and cups that allow the emblems to be prepared and passed to us in such a fitting and proper manner. And, I am always thankful when I see that those involved in the sacrament are dressed and groomed appropriately and that they have carefully washed and cleaned their hands prior to participating in the preparation, blessing, and passing of the sacrament.

(Note – It seems common sense to us today that small paper sacrament cups should not be washed and re-used, but the 1944 *General Handbook of Instructions*, published near the end of World

War II, included the guideline to Church leaders **that individual paper sacrament cups should only be used once and then discarded.** Apparently, some wards and branches weren't doing that.)

(Note – While I was writing this chapter, an article from the World Economic Forum appeared on the internet. **The article discussed how more than 170 nations have pledged to eliminate or significantly reduce single-use plastic items by the year 2030.** Several of the single-use items specifically mentioned in the article include **plastic cups,** grocery bags, straws, cutlery, and six-pack rings. This action by these countries will, no doubt, have an eventual impact on the Church's use of disposable individual plastic cups in our sacrament services.)

Sacrament Term

Injection Molding

Injection molding is the manufacturing process used in making the plastic bread and water trays that are currently available from the Church.

In a typical injection molding operation, granular plastic is fed into a heated barrel. After the plastic has melted, it is forced (injected) through a nozzle into a mold where the plastic takes the shape of the inside cavity of the mold. After the plastic cools, the mold is opened and the plastic shape is removed. The object is then trimmed and finished, as required. Injection molding is the most common modern method of manufacturing plastic parts.

The Church's bread tray consists of two parts – the white plastic base and the clear plastic handle. **Both parts are made by injection molding.** The water tray is made of three parts – the white base which acts as a receptacle for used cups, the clear handle, and the white lid which holds 36 individual cups of water. **All three parts are injection molded.**

Harper's Weekly and the Sacrament on Temple Square

Harper's Weekly **Visits Salt Lake City**

In 1871, having heard about the Mormon sacrament meetings that were held weekly in the Tabernacle on Temple Square, *Harper's Weekly* dispatched a reporter to Salt Lake City to write about them. **The September 30, 1871 issue of the magazine included an article and a large 16-inch by 23-inch, double-page, illustration of the sacrament meeting in the Tabernacle that was attended by the reporter.** (I have in my sacrament memorabilia collection an original copy of this 1871 magazine.) *Harper's Weekly*, which was published from 1857 until 1916, was a very popular and respected national periodical with more than a quarter million subscribers around that time. The caption for the illustration was, **"'SACRAMENT' IN THE MORMON TABERNACLE, SALT LAKE CITY, UTAH."** Here is the illustration that *Harper's* included in the issue:

A brief article about the sacrament meeting appeared on the page that followed the illustration. Under the heading, **"THE MORMON TABERNACLE,"** here is a portion of the article:

"The Mormon Temple, or Tabernacle, as the "faithful" prefer to call their sacred edifice, is a large, showy structure, of very little pretension to architectural beauty. It is 250 feet long, with many sandstone columns supporting the roof, the concave of which forms an unbroken arch. There is room enough in the interior to seat 8000 people. An immense organ is placed at the further end of the Tabernacle, just in front of it the pulpit, on either hand the choir seats, while a few steps below the platform is the dais where sit the elders and apostles of the church. The exercises comprise a prayer, a hymn, the administering of bread and water to the "faithful," and finally the sermon by BRIGHAM YOUNG. He speaks simply, plainly, and strongly. He loves, especially if there are gentiles present, to dilate upon the trials of his people, and their coming to their valley barefooted and naked; of their success, and the proofs that they were a chosen people – showing here, as in private, the strange magnetic influence which he yields with so much effect upon the minds of his disciples.

The double-page illustration which we give this week shows the administration of the "Sacrament," large pewter vessels, of which several may be seen in front of the pulpit, being used for the purpose. All present, men, women, children, and babies in arms, partake."

The Buildings on the Temple Block

Shortly after arriving in the Salt Lake Valley, Brigham Young designated a location on the north side of the valley as a future temple site. The ground surrounding this spot became known as the Temple Block, and was called this until after Salt Lake City was surveyed when it became known as Temple Square. Soon, the Church began erecting things on the site. **The first structure built there by the pioneers was a small bowery.** This bowery, the first of several boweries eventually built on the square, was a simple wooden framework covered with branches and bushes. It was used for religious meetings as well as social gatherings.

As the city's population grew, Brigham Young directed that a more permanent building – **to be known as a tabernacle** – be built on Temple Square. This building, **which was not the Tabernacle we know today,** was made of adobe bricks and was located in the area where the Assembly Hall now stands. **It was called the Adobe Tabernacle.** The building, 126 feet long and 64 feet wide, was completed in 1852 and seated 2,500 people. The Adobe Tabernacle housed an organ brought from Australia and was the home of a fledgling choir – a choir that grew over time and eventually became known as the Mormon Tabernacle Choir.

By the time the Adobe Tabernacle was completed, it was already too small, so the First Presidency undertook plans to build a larger tabernacle north of the Adobe Tabernacle. **The first meeting in this new and impressive domed building, the new Tabernacle, was the October 1867 general conference.** In 1877,

160

the Adobe Tabernacle was demolished and the Assembly Hall was built in its place.

Community Wide Sacrament Meetings

For many years, community wide sacrament meetings were held on Sundays on Temple Square – in the boweries, in the Adobe Tabernacle, and eventually in the new Tabernacle. On most Sundays, a sacrament meeting was held both in the morning and the afternoon. **Because the congregations were large, the sacrament was often blessed near the beginning of the meeting and then passed continually while the sermons were being preached and Church business was being conducted.** Bishops from around the valley, along with their counselors and other priesthood leaders, were assigned to administer and pass the sacrament.

Special Sacrament Vessels

You'll note that the *Harper's Weekly* article mentions that several large sacrament vessels were used in the administration of the sacrament in the Tabernacle. **Some of these sacrament goblets came into being because of an October 1852 invitation to the Saints by Brigham Young to have a special set of sacrament vessels crafted for use on Temple Square.** In that 1852 meeting, the Saints fully embraced the idea of a special sacrament service and a collection was taken up to accomplish this. **Members were quick to donate many of their personal silver items to the effort.** An excellent book, *The Tabernacle: An Old and Wonderful Friend*, by Scott Esplin, tells how a record was kept of the donations for the special Tabernacle sacrament set. Here is a summary of the donations:

- $149 in silver coin
- Several pounds of watch cases
- Spoons
- Rings

- Various other silver ornaments

These items were melted down and crafted into a special Tabernacle sacrament service **consisting of twelve solid silver sacrament water cups with double handles, twelve heavy silver plates for the bread, and several large water pitchers.** These sacrament vessels were used for many years for the sacrament meetings held on Temple Square – including for the sacrament meeting that was illustrated and described in the September 30, 1871 *Harper's Weekly* issue.

Temple Square Sacrament Meetings Phased Out

Eventually, as more and more wards in the Salt Lake area were able to construct their own meetinghouses, sacrament meetings on Temple Square were phased out. **The last sacrament meeting in the Tabernacle was held in 1894,** thus bringing to a close an interesting and important chapter in the history of the sacrament in the Church.

And what became of *Harper's Weekly*? After its final issue on May 13, 1916, it was absorbed by *The Independent* which in turn merged with *The Outlook* in 1918. Today, several periodicals with similar names – like *Harper's Magazine, Harper's Bazaar*, etc. – are still around.

(Note – The story is told that when Church members in St. George were discussing what kind of sacrament set they should buy, one good brother reported how Salt Lake got theirs. Quickly, the members in the area donated many of their silver possessions to the cause of crafting their own special silver sacrament service similar to what the Saints did up north.)

Sacrament Term

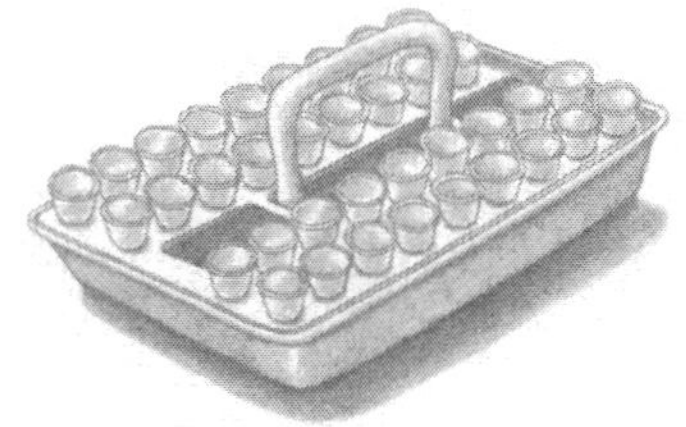

Transubstantiation

Transubstantiation is a term used in the Catholic Church for their belief that the bread and wine are transformed into the actual body and blood of Jesus Christ during the Eucharist (during their sacrament). According to the Catechism of the Catholic Church (the official book that defines the beliefs of the Catholic Church), "By the consecration of the bread and wine there takes place a change of the whole substance of the bread into the substance of the body of Christ our Lord and of the whole substance of the wine into the substance of his blood." They teach that the manner in which the change occurs is a mystery. They say that, "The signs of bread and wine become, in a way surpassing understanding, the Body and Blood of Christ."

In The Church of Jesus Christ of Latter-day Saints, we partake of the sacrament to remember the Savior's sacrifice of His flesh and blood and to renew sacred covenants. **We do not believe that the sacramental bread and water are changed into His actual body and blood.**

(Note – A related term, **consubstantiation**, is the belief by some faiths that the substance of the bread and wine **coexist** with the body and blood of Christ but do not actually change into the body and blood. They undergo a spiritual change but not a literal change.)

Officiating at the Sacred Desk

After three years of construction, **the Kirtland Temple was dedicated on Sunday, March 27, 1836.** Near the end of the daylong service, Joseph Smith read the dedicatory prayer, which was given to him by revelation (see Doctrine and Covenants 109), following which the choir sang *The Spirit of God*. **The sacrament was administered to those assembled,** several testimonies were borne, and then the congregation stood and rendered shouts of *Hosanna, Hosanna, Hosanna to God and the Lamb* near the conclusion of the service.

A formal dedicatory prayer, the singing of *The Spirit of God,* and the *Hosanna Shout* by all in attendance have characterized all temple dedications since.

One week later, **on April 3, which was Easter Sunday,** we read in the preface to Section 110 of the Doctrine and Covenants a quote from Joseph Smith about **the sacrament also being part** of the important meeting held in the temple that day:

"In the afternoon, **I assisted the other Presidents in distributing the Lord's Supper to the Church,** receiving it from the Twelve, whose privilege it was to officiate at **the sacred desk** this day. After having performed this service to my brethren, I retired to the pulpit, the veils being dropped, and bowed myself, with Oliver Cowdery, in solemn and silent prayer. After rising from prayer, the following vision was opened to both of us."

Section 110 of the Doctrine and Covenants then records the details of the marvelous manifestation and vision that Joseph Smith and Oliver Cowdery experienced. It was at that time that **Jesus Christ** appeared in glory to accept the Kirtland Temple as his house, that **Moses** and **Elias** appeared and committed the keys of their dispensations, and that **Elijah** returned to the earth and bestowed the keys of his dispensation, as was promised by Malachi in the Old Testament.

The sacred desk referred to in the quote from Joseph Smith was the **unique and symbolic sacrament table** located at the west end of the first-floor assembly room of the Kirtland Temple. **Shaped like the yoke of an ox team, the sacred desk was a drop-leaf table made of native black walnut wood stained dark.** Hinged on the top side, the table was designed so it could be raised up to a horizontal position and secured for the preparation of the sacrament. When not in use, it was folded down, revealing the large initials **"P.E.M."** which were inlaid twice in the top of the table. (These initials stood for **"Presidency Elders Melchizedek."**) Here is a photo of the **sacred desk:**

The **yoke shape** of the table is symbolic of the **yoke of Christ.** In Matthew 11:28-30, we read:

> "Come unto me, all ye that labour and are heavy laden, and I will give you rest. Take my **yoke** upon you, and learn of me; for I am meek and lowly in heart: and ye shall find rest unto your souls. **For my yoke is easy, and my burden is light."**

The design of the Kirtland Temple is interesting. Taller than most other buildings in the state of Ohio at that time, the original exterior of the building looked somewhat different than it does today. It had a gleaming red roof with a colorful bell tower and the exterior of the building was a sparkling bluish-gray stucco material. The building featured vibrant green entry doors and a number of ornate peaked Gothic windows were located on all four sides of the building. The glass in the small window panes of these windows was made by hand.

The first floor of the building was called the lower court. **It was designated for the sacrament, preaching, fasting, and praying.** At both ends of this large room were twelve ornately carved pulpits arranged in four rows of three pulpits each. The pulpits on the west end of the building were for the First Presidency and other Melchizedek Priesthood leaders. On the opposite end were similar pulpits designated for the bishopric and Aaronic Priesthood leaders. All of the pulpits, which were elevated and terraced, were accessible by flights of steps. Filling the middle part of the room were rows of pews which featured an adjustable design that allowed the congregation to face either end. A series of tall wooden columns from floor to ceiling ran the length of the room. Overhead were hung large canvas curtains designed to be rolled down between the pews to divide the space into temporary rooms.

The second floor of the temple contained another large assembly room, called the upper court, which was designed for education. Among other purposes, it was intended for the school of the prophets. The third-floor attic area had classrooms and offices. Joseph Smith's office was on this floor.

Temples and the Sacrament

The purpose of the Kirtland Temple was different than the purpose of today's temples. President Joseph Fielding Smith, in his book *Doctrines of Salvation,* Vol. 2, page 236, stated:

> "The purpose of the Kirtland Temple was not for performing saving ordinances but to provide a sanctuary where the Lord could send messengers from his presence to restore priesthood keys held in former dispensations, so that the work of gathering together all things in one in the dispensation of the fulness of times might go on."

In addition to the March 27 and April 3 instances, **the sacrament was periodically served in the Kirtland Temple** as members and Church leaders met there for various meetings and other purposes. When the Nauvoo Temple was built some years later, it also had two large assembly halls to accommodate special meetings and regular worship services for the Church members living in Nauvoo. **The sacrament was served as part of many of the meetings held in that temple.** And it was in the Nauvoo Temple where the first full saving ordinances were introduced, thus ushering in the most important function of our temples.

After arriving in the Salt Lake Valley, the Church began erecting temples whose primary purpose was to provide temple ordinances for the living and the deceased. Several of these temples, including the ones in St. George, Logan, Manti, and Salt Lake City, also had large assembly rooms where special meetings could be held. **The sacrament was served in many of those meetings.**

Because we now have meetinghouses throughout the world in which to gather for our sacrament services, today's temples do not need to function as meeting halls in which members come to partake of the sacrament. Rather, today's temples are specifically designed for temple ordinance work.

The Salt Lake Temple's Special Role

Because of its location at the headquarters of The Church of Jesus Christ of Latter-day Saints, the Salt Lake Temple is different in some of its functions from the other temples of the Church. In addition to the rooms in which ordinance work is performed, the Salt Lake Temple has several smaller meeting rooms on the fourth floor where the First Presidency, Quorum of the Twelve, and others can assemble for special meetings. **The sacrament is often part of those meetings.**

Additionally, on the top floor of the Salt Lake Temple is a **large assembly room.** With priesthood pulpits similar to those in the Kirtland Temple on each end of the hall, this room has been used over the years for a number of different purposes, including:

- **Solemn Assemblies** – Special meetings, often called solemn assemblies, have been held in this room. For instance, when I was serving in a bishopric in a Salt Lake City ward, the leaders of the Church invited members of stake presidencies and bishoprics in a number of stakes to come to a special meeting, which they called a solemn assembly. The meeting was held in the Salt Lake Temple on a Sunday morning. At this meeting, held in the large room on the 5th floor, **we partook of the sacrament** and received special counsel pertaining to our callings.
- **Special Teaching** – In 1966, as a 19-year-old going on a mission to the Southern Far East Mission, I spent a week in the Salt Lake Mission Home, which was located in an old school building a block from Temple Square. (This was before the era of Language Training Missions and Missionary Training Centers.) During our stay in the Mission Home, our group of 326 missionaries was invited to a meeting in the Salt Lake Temple. We met in the large assembly room on the 5th floor and spent several wonderful hours being taught about the gospel and about missionary work by Elder Harold B. Lee of the Quorum of the Twelve. During the last part of the meeting, he invited us to ask

questions about the temple or anything else we wondered about. He very graciously and patiently answered our questions. **The sacrament was not served at this meeting.**

- **Other Purposes** – From time to time, this room has been used for other sacred purposes, as seen fit by the First Presidency. For instance, in the early 1950s, President Gordon B. Hinckley, then working as the executive secretary of the General Missionary Committee, was assigned by the First Presidency to chair a committee to prepare a special film – **the first film to be used in a temple** – for the new Swiss Temple. (The Swiss Temple, which was dedicated in 1955, was the first temple located outside of North America.) Because the temple would serve Saints speaking a number of different languages, the film was designed so that it could be dubbed in multiple languages. President Hinckley often talked about his experiences in producing the film and how it was largely prepared in the assembly room on the fifth floor of the Salt Lake Temple.

Conclusion

Although the sacrament has been served at times in some of our temples over the years, it is not usually part of how temples are now used. Instead, **we go to our local meetinghouses,** which have been specially designed and dedicated to help us participate in the sacred sacrament ordinance.

(Note – Following are several additional things about the Kirtland Temple that I found to be interesting:

- **Stucco – The bluish-gray stucco** on the exterior of the original temple sparkled thanks to the women and children of Kirtland who contributed discarded shards of crockery, glass, and china to the construction effort. These items were ground up and added to the stucco mixture, providing a beautiful glint to the exterior of the building. Today, the exterior of the Kirtland Temple has been painted white and the bluish-gray stucco is no longer visible.

- **Windows** – There are **over 3,500 individual hand-made glass window panes** in the building's many Gothic-style windows. This early type of glass had waves and imperfections in it which made it rather difficult to see through clearly. This characteristic of hand-made glass was a big enough visual factor that some states enacted laws that disqualified a witness's testimony at a court trial if the witness was testifying that they saw something take place while they were looking through a glass window.

- **Drop-down Curtains** – In order to create private spaces in the large assembly room on the first floor, **drop-down canvas curtains, referred to as veils, were hung from the ceiling.** Ropes and pulleys were used to lower and raise them. During the Saints' exodus from Kirtland, some of the curtains were removed from the building and used as covers for **"prairie schooners" (covered wagons).** The remaining ones were eventually taken down due to local laws being enacted which required curtains such as these to be made of fire-resistant material (such as asbestos), which would have made replacement curtains too heavy to be practical. Years later, some of the original rods and pieces of curtain were found stored in the basement of the temple.

- **Original Materials** – During the time when the temple was practically abandoned after the exodus of the Saints, **vandals and souvenir hunters carried away some of the ornamentation of the pulpits and stairways and destroyed the communion table.** Later on, renovations to the building restored and replaced most of these items – so some of the things you now see when visiting the building, including the **ox yoke-shaped sacred desk,** are not original.

- **Native Woods** - Several types of wood native to the Kirtland area were used in the construction of the temple. Black walnut was used for the sacrament table and stair railings, while white walnut was used for the pulpits, pews, and ornamental woodwork.

- **Ceiling Space** – To create a sound buffer between the first and second floor assembly rooms, a larger than normal dead air space was created between the ceiling of the first floor and the floor of the second floor. In some areas of the ceiling, the space was as much as five feet.
- **Grooved Columns** – The large flutes (grooves) in the floor-to-ceiling columns in the first-floor assembly room were made with the help of ox teams. Large metal planes were attached to **ox yokes** and then drawn by the animals along the wood in order to make the deep grooves.

Some of this additional information about the Kirtland Temple comes from a wonderful article titled *Some Little-known Facts About a Well-known Building*. It was written in 1925 by C. Edward Miller who was a church historian for The Reorganized Church of Jesus Christ of Latter Day Saints (now called The Community of Christ). The Community of Christ is the present owner of the building.)

Sacrament Term

Maundy Thursday

On the occasion of the Last Supper, we read in John 13:1-17 that the Savior girded himself with a towel, poured water into a basin, and washed and wiped the feet of the apostles. **The washing of the apostles' feet by Christ was a profound gesture of service and humility, emphasizing the principle that whoever would be a leader among men must also be a servant.**

This same ordinance of washing feet was part of the restoration of all things and has been participated in by leaders of our Church on certain sacred occasions in this dispensation. **Early instances where this took place were at the school of the prophets in 1833 and in the Kirtland Temple in 1836.**

Other Christian churches also participate in the rite of foot washing. You perhaps have heard of **Maundy Thursday,** which is a holy day celebrated by a number of denominations. **Traditionally falling on the Thursday before Easter, Maundy Thursday is the day on which they commemorate Christ's washing of the apostles' feet during the Last Supper.** Maundy is the term for the rite of foot washing. Although opinions on the origin of the word differ, many experts say that maundy comes from a Latin word meaning a mandate from God to serve.

(Note – The ordinance of washing feet is mentioned in Doctrine and Covenants 88:139-141. It is not found in the Book of Mormon.)

Absolute Quiet – The Ideal Condition

On May 2, 1946, the First Presidency (Presidents George Albert Smith; J. Reuben Clark, Jr.; and David O. McKay) issued an important letter to stake presidents and bishops concerning the sacrament. The purpose of the letter was to "recommend" to the Church that there should be no music during the sacrament and that **the ideal condition was to have absolute quiet during this time.** Here is a portion of that letter:

"Dear Brethren:

Inquiries received at the office of the First Presidency disclose the fact that there is a divergence of opinion and varied practices among ward officers with respect to the kind of music, if any, that should be rendered during the administration of the sacrament.

Recently the question came before the First Presidency and the Twelve who unanimously approved the recommendation that **the ideal condition is to have absolute quiet** during the passing of the sacrament, and that we look with disfavor upon vocal solos, duets, group singing, or instrumental music during the administration of this sacred ordinance.

There is no objection to having appropriate music during the preparation of the emblems, but after the prayer is offered, **perfect silence should prevail** until the bread and water have been partaken of by the full congregation."

Over the years in many wards and branches, a number of different practices and procedures had become part of the sacrament ordinance. The intent of the First Presidency's letter was to eliminate the various opinions concerning the sacrament and to create a uniform Church-wide policy for conducting the ordinance. **The First Presidency's "recommendation" was taken to heart by Church leaders and members and since 1946 the policy of the Church has been to have absolute quiet during the passing of the sacrament.**

In the early days of the Church, the blessing and passing of the sacrament often took a long time, primarily because the congregations drank from communal goblets rather than from individual sacrament cups. **In those meetings, as mentioned previously in this book, it became common practice to have the passing of the sacrament take place in the background as speakers spoke, musical numbers were presented, and even while Church business was conducted.** Later, as individual cups were introduced and the sacrament portion of the meeting took up less time, **music of some sort often continued to be used before, during, and after the ordinance.** For example, my father told me that when he was young, trumpets heralded the beginning of the sacrament in his ward and that his good friends, Percy and Leona, sometimes played musical duets on the violin and cello while the sacrament was being passed.

Elder L. Tom Perry, in an April 2006 general conference address, emphasized the Church's policy about the importance of silence during the sacrament when he said:

"The sacrament is one of the most sacred ordinances in the Church. Partaking of the sacrament worthily gives us an opportunity for spiritual growth. I remember that when I was a child, beautiful music was played during the passing of the sacrament. **The Brethren soon asked us to stop that practice because our minds were centered on the music rather than on the atoning sacrifice of our Lord and Savior.** During the administration of the sacrament, we set aside the world. It is a period of spiritual renewal."

Personally, I am grateful for the special few minutes each week that are available for us to put aside the things of the world and to focus exclusively on the Savior and his Atonement. **This weekly period of absolute quiet is a precious gift from Heavenly Father** and I am going to do my best to make better use of this gift and to block out all distractions and outside thoughts during the sacrament.

(Note – While serving in the Primary, my wife would use the following little story to help Primary children understand the importance of being quiet and reverent during the sacrament:)

A Thief in Church
(Adapted from a story by Mildred N. Hoyer)

Are you a thief in church?

It happened last Sunday – and then again this Sunday. **There was a thief in our sacrament meeting.** Not a thief who took money, jewelry, and possessions, but a thief who stole something much more valuable. **This thief stole silence!** While I was trying to ponder the Atonement and focus on the Savior during the sacrament, this thief was sitting on the row behind me whispering, squirming, tapping feet, playing with a phone, and rattling papers.

I'm sure this person doesn't see themself as a thief and doesn't think they're doing much harm, but to me and to those around me, this thief was a distraction. **This thief stole our silence – and silence is something very sacred and precious during the sacrament.**

Are you a thief in church?

Sacrament Term

Thermoforming

Thermoforming is the manufacturing process the Church uses to make its small individual plastic sacrament cups (see Chapter 19).

To produce the cups, thin plastic sheeting from a large roll is fed into one end of a large thermoforming machine. As the sheeting enters, it is heated to a pliable temperature and then the individual three-dimensional cups are formed on a mold. The cups are then trimmed, cooled, stacked, and packaged. The plastic sheeting, now with many holes punched in it, travels out the other end of the machine where it is wound onto a take-up reel for recycling.

In the case of the Church's sacrament cups, the thin plastic sheeting used in the thermoforming process is food-grade plastic that is 0.17 mm in thickness.

A Special Collection

**"When there is proper regard for the past and its people,
we enrich the present as well as the future."
- President Spencer W. Kimball**

I love a good museum and have been able to visit quite a few remarkable ones during my lifetime. If you asked me to list several of my favorites, I would probably pick:

- **The National Air and Space Museum in Washington, D.C.** – Part of the vast Smithsonian Institution, this fascinating museum is full of things that interest me and catch my attention. I especially like the Wright Flyer airplane, the Apollo 11 command module, and the old Spirit of St. Louis plane.
- **The Sistine Chapel Portion of the Vatican Museums** – I marvel at the beautiful ceiling of the famous Sistine Chapel which can be viewed while visiting the Vatican Museums. For centuries, the Sistine Chapel has been the site of papal conclaves that elect new popes. Michelangelo's frescoes that adorn the chapel's ceiling and walls are truly stunning!
- **Le Louvre in Paris** – For me, it doesn't get much better than this vast museum that houses some of the most famous

artwork in the world – such as the Mona Lisa, Winged Victory, and Venus de Milo.

- **The Rijksmuseum in Amsterdam** – I first visited this museum as a young six-year-old boy and have loved it ever since. Among my favorite paintings in the museum are *The Night Watch* by Rembrandt and *Windmill at Wijk bij Duurstede* by van Ruisdael. We have a large Delft Blue plate of the van Ruisdael painting hanging on the wall of our living room.

- **The Hong Kong Museum of History** – Located on the Kowloon side of the harbor, this museum has amazing exhibits that tell the story of Hong Kong, one of my favorite cities.   I particularly love seeing the way the New Territories used to be, the displays depicting British life in the early days of the colony, and the old junks and rickshaws that were an important part of Hong Kong's past.

And I would also put the Church History Museum in downtown Salt Lake City on that list. I love our Latter-day Saint heritage and am especially drawn to the history of the sacrament in our Church. The Church History Museum typically has on display some wonderful old sacrament trays and sacrament vessels that add interesting insight into the development of the sacrament in this dispensation. **As an example, a special exhibit a few years ago featured a beautiful glass sacramental goblet with a gold pattern around the brim that came from the original Nauvoo Temple.   The display also included an impressive eight-piece silver sacrament service with four large ornate cups used many years ago in a small ward in northern Utah.**

As is the case with many of the other types of artifacts that are put on display in the Church History Museum, the sacrament items are changed from time to time. They are brought out and become part of an interesting exhibit for a while, and then the presentation is dismantled and the items disappear.

So, where do these valuable sacrament artifacts go after they are no longer on display – and how many old sacrament

items does the Church have? Well, the answers to these questions are the focus of the rest of this chapter.

The Church History Museum has a collection of **more than 150,000 artifacts of all kinds** that tell the story of The Church of Jesus Christ of Latter-day Saints from its earliest beginnings to the present time. Consisting of display areas on several floors, a conservation lab, offices, and a museum store, the museum also has **a limited-access basement area** to house many of the items that cannot be on public display due to space limitations. (There is also an off-site warehouse to accommodate additional items in the Church's vast collection.) The present museum was opened in 1984 and has been remodeled and updated several times since then.

As with other state-of-the art museums, **special care is taken in regard to temperature, humidity, air quality, and lighting to ensure that the items in the museum are carefully protected against damage and deterioration.** The Church's collection consists of a variety of historical objects – paintings, tapestries, statues, sculptures, furniture, clothing, personal belongings, tools, stonework, books, photos, musical instruments, stained-glass windows – **and sacrament memorabilia**.

The hundreds of sacrament memorabilia items are of particular interest to me. Except for the ones that are on public display from time to time, **the sacrament items are housed in special cabinets in their own section of the private basement storage area of the museum, with many of the items kept in protective containers and boxes.** Before handling any of the artifacts, rubber or cloth gloves must be worn to keep skin oils from touching them.

The wonderful sacrament collection in the museum is extensive, consisting of water trays, bread trays, goblets, pitchers, cups, platters, baskets, water filling devices, and sacrament table cloths. A number of different natural and man-made materials were used in the making of the items – steel, stainless steel, pewter, tin, wood, wicker, ceramics, glass, fabric, paper, and plastic. Some date back to the very early days of the Church and, as a group, the collection helps tell the remarkable story of the growth of the Church and the way the sacrament ordinance has evolved to keep pace with that growth.

The process of serving the sacrament to members of the Church has changed over time. As sacrament memorabilia is studied, interesting stories unfold concerning the modification of the ordinance. These stories bless our lives, help lead us to a greater love for the sacrament, and aid us in acquiring a more complete understanding of the Atonement and the sacrament ordinance.

(Note – The Daughters of Utah Pioneer Museum at 300 N. Main in Salt Lake City also has an interesting display of sacrament memorabilia.)

**"Preserve your memories, keep them well;
What you forget, you can never retell."
- Louisa May Alcott**

Sacrament Term

Holy Chalice

In Christian tradition, the vessel that Jesus Christ used at the Last Supper to serve the wine is known as the Holy Chalice. By definition, a chalice is a cup or goblet. According to some beliefs, after the crucifixion of Christ, Peter took the cup with him to Rome. After Peter's martyrdom in Rome, legend has it that the cup was passed on to Peter's successors and eventually to others. There are many traditions concerning the chalice's present location, such as one that says that it is housed in a cathedral in Spain.

The cup that was used at the Last Supper has become the subject of much Christian folklore and legend, **but no true reliable information exists concerning it.**

(Note – In some books, movies, and plays, (such as *The Da Vinci Code*, *Indiana Jones and the Last Crusade*, and *Monty Python and the Holy Grail*) the Holy Chalice is referred to as the **Holy Grail.**)

Church Magazine Ads and the Sacrament

As I was growing up on Beverly Street in Salt Lake City, I loved to read the magazines that came into our home. My favorite was *Boy's Life*, which was my own personal subscription, and which I always read cover to cover as soon as it arrived each month. Published by the Boy Scouts of America, **it had fun regular features like the Pee Wee Harris comic strip** (Pee Wee was a young Boy Scout who always seemed to get into mischief), **Pedro the Mailburro** (Pedro was a donkey that answered readers' mail), and **Think and Grin** (jokes submitted by Scouts, such as the following: Eagle Scout: "Why were the Scouts so tired on April 1?" Tenderfoot Scout: "You got me." Eagle Scout: "Because they had just finished a 31-day March.") I also really liked the ads that were scattered throughout the magazine, such as those from:

- U. S. Keds – the shoe of champions
- Schwinn – the bike hiker's favorite bicycle
- Louisville Slugger baseball bats – leaders in the hit parade
- Tootsie Roll – the perfect candy (delicious, wholesome, chocolaty flavor)
- Kodak – cameras fit for every boy's adventure

After devouring *Boy's Life*, I also enjoyed the other magazines that arrived in our home, like the *Saturday Evening Post*, the *Children's Friend*, the *Improvement Era* – and even my mother's *Reader's Digest*.

As I was studying the history of the sacrament, **I was reminded that Church magazines used to carry advertising, including ads for sacrament-related items. The ads helped subsidize the costs of the periodicals.** An example of such a magazine was **the June 1912 issue of the *Improvement Era* which carried 15 ads,** including ones from the following entities:

- Jos. Wm. Taylor – Utah's leading undertaker and licensed embalmer
- Consolidated Wagon & Machine Co. – dependable farm implements
- West's Mail Order House – L.D.S. knitted garments suitable for warm weather, fine weave, light weight, bleached, per pair…71c
- Denver & Rio Grande Railroad – Pullman sleepers from Salt Lake City to Denver, St. Louis, and Chicago
- Heber J. Grant & Co. – home fire insurance
- Koffe-et – three weeks of Koffe-et will cure you of the coffee habit, your grocer sells it, 25c a package
- Commercial Savings Benefit Co. – 6% per annum interest on deposits
- Deseret Farmer Newspaper – the farm paper of today and tomorrow, published every week fifty-two times a year for only one dollar per year, a set of six Oxford silver plate spoons free to all who pay in advance

Along with these ads, the June 1912 issue carried the following full-page sacrament-related advertisement placed by the Deseret Sunday School Union Book Store, the exclusive sales agent for the new sacrament service:

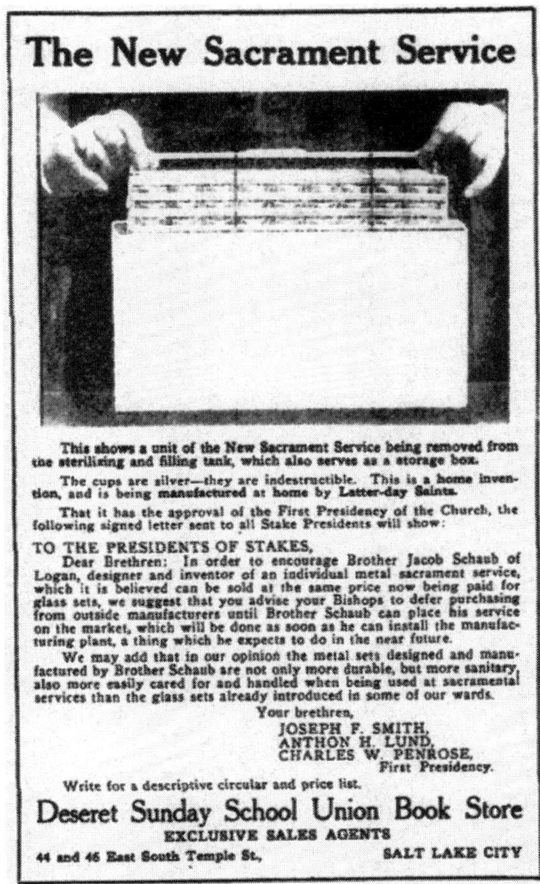

This shows a unit of the New Sacrament Service being removed from the sterilizing and filling tank, which also serves as a storage box.

The cups are silver—they are indestructible. This is a home invention, and is being manufactured at home by Latter-day Saints.

That it has the approval of the First Presidency of the Church, the following signed letter sent to all Stake Presidents will show:

TO THE PRESIDENTS OF STAKES,

Dear Brethren: In order to encourage Brother Jacob Schaub of Logan, designer and inventor of an individual metal sacrament service, which it is believed can be sold at the same price now being paid for glass sets, we suggest that you advise your Bishops to defer purchasing from outside manufacturers until Brother Schaub can place his service on the market, which will be done as soon as he can install the manufacturing plant, a thing which he expects to do in the near future.

We may add that in our opinion the metal sets designed and manufactured by Brother Schaub are not only more durable, but more sanitary, also more easily cared for and handled when being used at sacramental services than the glass sets already introduced in some of our wards.

Your brethren,
JOSEPH F. SMITH,
ANTHON H. LUND,
CHARLES W. PENROSE,
First Presidency.

Write for a descriptive circular and price list.

Deseret Sunday School Union Book Store

EXCLUSIVE SALES AGENTS

44 and 46 East South Temple St., SALT LAKE CITY

As far as I can determine, this was the very first Church magazine ad that was devoted to a sacrament item. As mentioned earlier in the book, the very first time individual sacrament cups were used in the Church was on June 18, 1911 in the Salt Lake 18th Ward. **This event spawned a new industry in the Church – the industry of making individual sacrament cups and of making trays to hold those sacrament cups.** It also prompted Latter-day Saint members with a creative bent to invent devices, such as the one shown in the foregoing ad, to fill the cups and to come up with ways to clean and sanitize them after they had been used.

A significant part of the ad was the unusual endorsement the device's maker, Jacob Schaub, (who was discussed earlier in the book) received from the First Presidency:

That it has the approval of the First Presidency of the Church, the following signed letter sent to all Stake Presidents will show:

TO THE PRESIDENTS OF STAKES,

Dear Brethren: In order to encourage Brother Jacob Schaub of Logan, designer and inventor of an individual metal sacrament service, which it is believed can be sold at the same price now being paid for glass sets, we suggest that you advise your Bishops to defer purchasing from outside manufacturers until Brother Schaub can place his service on the market, which will be done as soon as he can install the manufacturing plant, a thing which he expects to do in the near future.

We may add that in our opinion the metal sets designed and manufactured by Brother Schaub are not only more durable, but more sanitary, also more easily cared for and handled when being used at sacramental services than the glass sets already introduced in some of our wards.

Your brethren,
JOSEPH F. SMITH,
ANTHON H. LUND,
CHARLES W. PENROSE,
First Presidency

This Jacob Schaub sterilizing and filling tank was popular for a number of years, but in the long run **disposable individual sacrament cups made of paper and plastic took over.** Cleaning and sanitizing devices for cups were no longer needed.

A sacrament tray ad in the September 1925 issue of the *Improvement Era,* was placed by the Bureau of Information, which was located on the "Temple Block." (Do you remember the Bureau of Information situated just inside the south gate of Temple Square? The first bureau, a small octagonal booth, was built in 1902. It was replaced in 1904 by a larger building that included a Church history museum, and in 1966 by a full visitors' center.) This somewhat-blurry 1925 ad promoted the "BEST IN THE MARKET" sacrament tray and glass sacrament cups.

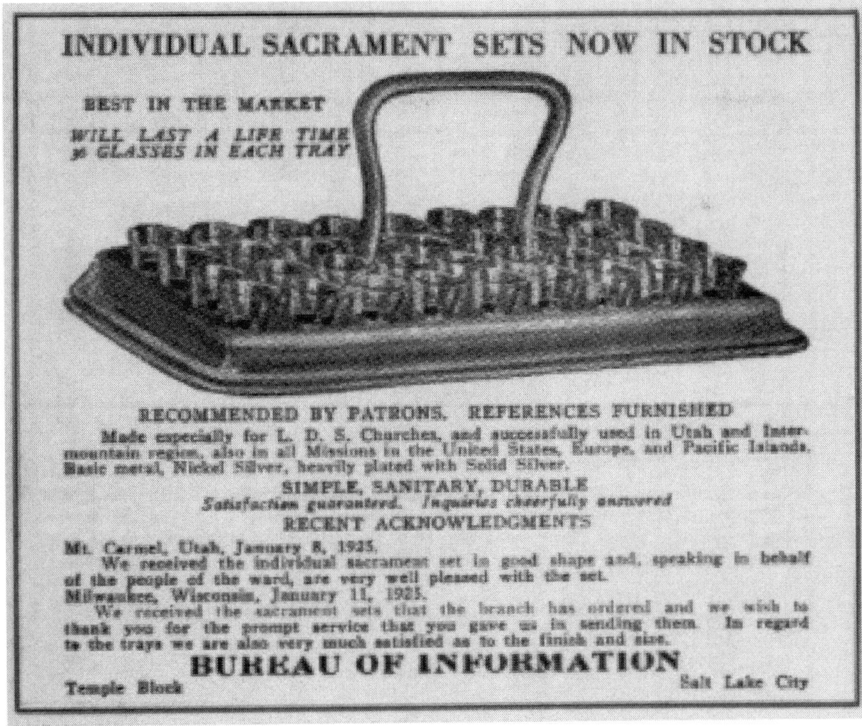

The heading of the ad read "INDIVIDUAL SACRAMENT SETS NOW IN STOCK." Concerning the metal water tray, it said that it "WILL LAST A LIFE TIME, 36 GLASSES IN EACH TRAY." The advertisement also carried two endorsements, one from a ward in Mt. Carmel, Utah and one from a branch in Milwaukee, Wisconsin.

Even non-Church entities placed sacrament ads in Church magazines, such as the following one by the **Daynes Jewelry Company** in the April 1930 *Improvement Era*. It promoted an improved sanitary sacrament set. **The difficult-to-read copy in the ad mentions that there is a free trial offer for both a round metal tray with 36 glasses and a patented instantaneous filler.**

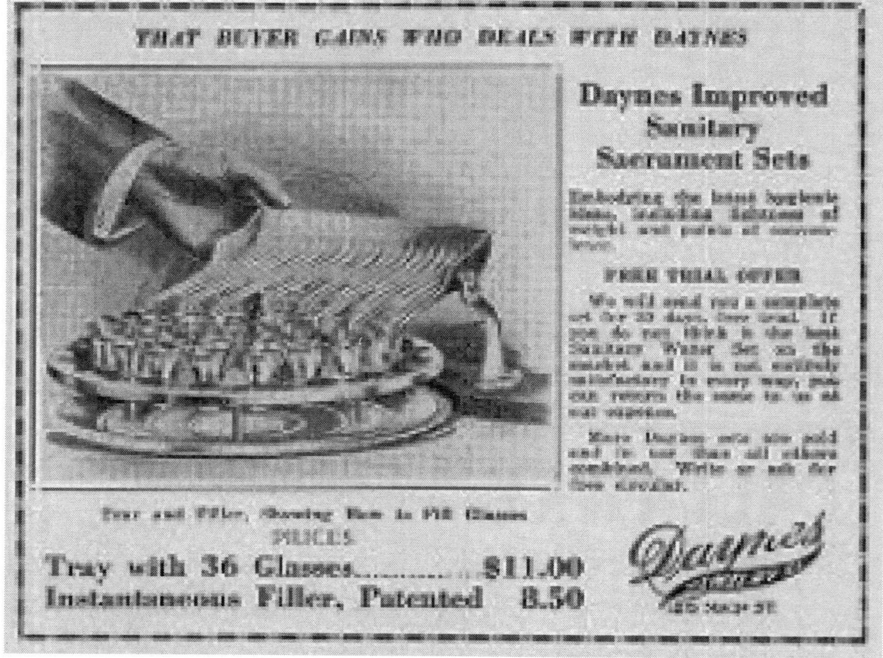

Conclusion

The advertisements shown in this chapter are just a few of the sacrament-related ads that appeared in Church magazines over the years. They helped wards and branches keep up to date with new designs and improvements in sacrament trays and other sacrament items. **Eventually, ads were no longer needed as the purchasing of sacrament trays, cups, and related items became centralized, with Church units buying what they needed directly from the Church.**

From the earliest days of the Church, magazines have been a great blessing to members. In August 2020, the First Presidency said, **"Church magazines are a valuable resource for learning about the gospel of Jesus Christ and feeling a sense of belonging to His Church. Our desire is that members everywhere will**

subscribe and welcome this faith-sustaining influence into their hearts and homes."

(Note - For informational purposes, following is a recap of the main magazines the Church has published over the years:

Prior to 1971
- *The Juvenile Instructor* – 1866 to 1929
  - This was the first children's magazine published between the Mississippi River and the West Coast. It was privately owned until 1901 when the Church acquired it.
- *The Improvement Era* – 1897 to 1970
  - During these years, it was the official publication for a variety of Church organizations, including the Seventies, the Young Men's Mutual Improvement Association, the Young Ladies' Mutual Improvement Association, priesthood quorums, Church schools, the Church Music Committee, and the Home Teaching Committee.
- *The Children's Friend* – 1902 to 1970
  - For children aged approximately three through twelve. In addition to appearing in print, some stories from the magazine were dramatized for a number of years for a radio program called *The Children's Friend on the Air.* Does anyone remember those?
- *The Relief Society Magazine* – 1915 to 1970
  - For its entire 55 years, the *Relief Society Magazine* was owned and operated by the General Board of the Relief Society, not by the Church, as such. All of the editors were women.
- *The Instructor* – 1930 to 1970
  - The official publication of the Sunday School, this magazine was specially created for the many teachers in the Church.

192

1971 to 2020 – In 1971, the Church consolidated its English-language periodicals.

- ***The Ensign***
  - Aimed at adult members of the Church, the full title of this magazine was *The Ensign of The Church of Jesus Christ of Latter-day Saints*. Each May and November issue carried the proceedings of the Church's semi-annual general conferences.
- ***The New Era***
  - Geared towards the youth of the Church, for some years a special feature of each month's *New Era* was a Mormonad, a clever full-page advertisement promoting gospel ideals. Poster-size versions of the ads were made available to wards and branches to put up on the bulletin boards in meetinghouses.
- ***The Friend***
  - Created for the Primary-aged children of the Church, each magazine included messages from Church leaders, activities, artwork, crafts, and stories.

In 1977

- ***The Liahona*** – From 1977
  - Begun as a Spanish-language periodical, the *Liahona* evolved to become the international magazine for non-English speaking members of all ages.

2021 to Present – Beginning in January 2021, the Church replaced its four previous magazines with three global magazines.

- ***The Liahona***
  - The updated and revised *Liahona* replaced the *Ensign* as the worldwide magazine for all adult members. It is published in multiple languages.
- ***For the Strength of Youth***
  - This new magazine replaced the *New Era*, becoming the global youth magazine of the Church.

- ***The Friend***
    - This long-time periodical was expanded and revised to become the Church's international magazine for children.)

Sacrament Term

Intinction

Practiced by some faiths, **intinction** is a method of partaking of the sacrament in which **the sacrament wafer (or piece of bread) is dipped into the sacrament wine (or water) before it is consumed.** This allows the recipient to receive both elements of the sacrament together at the same time. Those who practice intinction feel this manner of partaking of the sacramental elements helps them achieve a closer unity with Christ.

In some churches, the dipping is done by the priest or minister and in others by the communicants themselves. The practice of **intinction** appears to date back to the 4th century A.D. **The Church of Jesus Christ of Latter-day Saints does not follow this practice.**

The Most Significant Sacrament Changes

For the final chapter of the book, let me summarize what I think have been the most significant changes in the sacrament ordinance in the nearly 200 years since The Church of Jesus Christ of Latter-day Saints was restored:

1. **Partaking of the sacrament weekly** – Rather than being a sporadic event as it sometimes was early on, sacrament meetings and the partaking of the sacrament are now an important weekly occurrence throughout the Church.
2. **Using the sacrament prayers found in the scriptures** – These prayers, which are to be read word for word, are now used each time the sacrament is blessed.
3. **Water instead of wine** – Water is now the approved substance used in the sacrament ordinance.
4. **Individual sacrament cups** – These have replaced communal goblets.
5. **The involvement of young men** – Young Aaronic Priesthood holders, rather than older men, now normally handle the preparation, blessing, and passing of the sacrament.

6. **Uniform sacrament policies and procedures** – The policies and procedures for holding a sacrament meeting and conducting the sacrament ordinance are now uniform throughout the Church.

7. **Natural and not formal** – The passing of the sacrament should be natural and not overly formal. Dressing and acting alike, or in a rigid military manner, are not required.

8. **Meetinghouse design** – The important role of the sacrament ordinance is reflected in the design of today's meetinghouses.

9. **Once each Sabbath day** – The sacrament is now offered just one time each Sabbath day, rather than twice as was done for many years when we also partook of the sacrament in Sunday School.

10. **Silence** – Instead of having music or talks from the pulpit during the ordinance, we now strive for quiet reverence while partaking of the sacrament.

11. **Disposable sacrament cups** – Inexpensive and lightweight disposable sacrament cups have replaced ones that needed to be washed after each use.

12. **Sacrament in homes** – Under certain circumstances (such as during a pandemic), families and individuals have now been authorized to hold sacrament meetings and partake of the sacrament in their homes.

As taught by President Russell M. Nelson on a number of occasions, the restoration of The Church of Jesus Christ of Latter-day Saints was not a single event. It is a process that is still continuing today. While on a Church tour in South America in October 2018, he said:

"We are witnesses to a process of restoration. If you think the Church has been fully restored, you're just seeing the beginning. There is much more to come. Wait till next year. And then the next year. Eat your vitamin pills. Get your rest. It's going to be exciting."

I am grateful to be a member of The Church of Jesus Christ of Latter-day Saints and to live in these interesting and important times, and I can't wait to see what changes in the Church may come next – perhaps even additional ones pertaining to the ordinance of the sacrament.

Sacrament Term

When I Drink it New

The scriptures tell us about **a future meeting** when **"Christ and His servants from all dispensations are to partake of the sacrament."** (See the introductory explanation to verses 5-14 in Doctrine and Covenants Section 27.)

When speaking to His apostles at the conclusion of the Last Supper, Christ said:

"But I say unto you, I will not drink henceforth of this fruit of the vine, until that day **when I drink it new** with you in my Father's kingdom." (Matthew 26:29)

And in Doctrine and Covenants Section 27, we read that the Savior said the following to the Prophet Joseph Smith:

"…for the hour cometh that **I will drink of the fruit of the vine** with you on the earth…" (Doctrine and Covenants 27:5)

These scriptures inform us that **the Savior will partake of the sacrament** with His apostles and others in a special meeting that is to take place **on this earth when He returns again.** Doctrine and Covenants 27 then goes on to specifically mention that the following individuals will be among those who will join Him in this meeting: **Moroni, Elias, John (the Baptist), Elijah, Joseph, Jacob, Isaac, Abraham, Michael (Adam), Peter, James, and John.**

About the Author

Born in Salt Lake City, Utah, Lee H. Van Dam has also lived in The Netherlands and Hong Kong. He holds an MBA degree and is the owner of a real estate management, sales, and consulting firm.

Lee and his wife, Holly, are the parents of two children and they have seven grandchildren. They love to travel and Lee enjoys playing golf. *The Sacrament – A Historical View* is his fourth book.